SCREW IT
Let's do lunch!

SCREW IT
Let's do lunch!

David Bullard

Sunday Times

MACMILLAN

First published in 2007
by Pan Macmillan South Africa
Private Bag X19, Northlands, 2116
www.panmacmillan.co.za

Reprinted 2007 (twice), 2008

ISBN 978-1-77010-073-2

Royalties from the sale of this book will be donated to charity.

Cover illustration by Dov Fedler
Cover design and typesetting: Triple M Design
Printed and bound in South Africa by Pinetown Printers

Contents

2006

Acknowledgements

To Mary-Anne Pillay for electronically gathering the columns
in the book.

To Dov Fedler for a great cover.

To the doctors, nurses and staff at the Milpark Hospital Trauma Unit
for looking after me.

To the Parkview Police for their professionalism.

To the murderous thug who shot me for managing to miss
every vital organ.

To the many family, friends and followers of the column who
sent their good wishes.

To the *Sunday Times* for continuing to offer me space every week.

To Pan Macmillan for publishing me.

To Jacquie Bullard for putting up with all my nonsense.

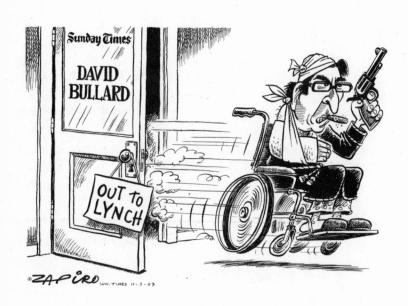

Introduction

A couple of years have passed since the publication of *Out to Lunch Again* and I know that the more intelligent members of the public will be clamouring once again for something to slip into a Christmas stocking or to give to a special friend, which is why we've lovingly collected together the columns from the past two years, printed them on the finest paper and elegantly bound them within a lavishly illustrated cover.

This is the final volume to make up the highly collectible *Out to Lunch* trilogy and you will notice two things. Firstly, I have an enthusiastic new publisher and, secondly, we have deliberately gone for a more original title than *Out to Lunch Again Again*.

As we go to press I have a defamation case looming and a 9mm bullet in my pelvis. The defamation case is courtesy of one Jacob Zuma who feels his dignity has been damaged by an article I wrote. He clearly hasn't a clue what journalists earn because he's suing me for R6 million. The bullet is courtesy of an intruder who dropped in to my home unannounced with two friends on 7 March 2007, and demanded money and guns. Unfortunately I wasn't in a generous mood that evening and decided to hit the panic button. That didn't sit well with the three thugs, and so they shot me in the stomach and left me for dead. Fortunately the bullet passed through my arm without doing any damage, and then entered my abdomen and travelled all the way to a few millimetres from my spine, also without hitting anything important or doing any serious damage. As one reader wrote, 'this confirms what we've known all along, you've got no guts'.

I'm often told that I've had a dreadful 2007 but I'm not so sure. If I'd been killed or badly injured I might agree but surviving an assassination attempt unscathed is good news in my book. Similarly, the opportunity to defend media freedom is something to be relished rather than dreaded.

We are privileged to live in a society where freedom of expression is allowed. Some politicians make no secret of the fact that they would like to impose a code of conduct (censorship, in other words) on the media but most of our public figures are intelligent enough to know that they are likely to be mocked by editors, columnists and cartoonists if they step out of line. That's a sign of a vigorous democracy. When politicians become vocal about wanting to permanently silence those who criticise them or highlight their shortcomings then we should be worried. I believe figures in public life should expect public scrutiny but I would because that's how I make my living. Without people like Jacob Zuma, I would have nothing to write about.

The *Out to Lunch* column celebrates its 14th birthday in 2008 and I'm rather hoping it will make its 15th and even its 16th. I'm certain that our politicians will continue to provide a rich source for material in the years to come. Whether I will continue to be free to write about them is no longer quite so certain.

David Bullard
5 July 2007

Zuma goes from the frying pan into fire

26 June 2005

I can't think of anything worse than spending day after day in a gloomy courtroom, having my financial peccadilloes exposed to the obvious delight of the media. Apart from the tedium of legal procedure and the unwelcome publicity, there are also the costs to think about.

But this is precisely what Jacob Zuma wished for and his wish has now been granted by the National Prosecuting Authority (NPA), which wants him to respond to two charges of corruption.

Good defence lawyers don't come cheap and Zuma's financial affairs are known to be chaotic – so one wonders who will be paying for his defence team.

If I were Zuma I would have cut my losses after the outcome of the Schabir Shaik trial and opted for a quiet retirement in rural KwaZulu-Natal, but clearly all that talk about being found guilty by the media has affected his judgment.

For the next few months the investigators will be digging away, going through Zuma's accounts and checking whether his personal relationships were tainted by corruption. Only then, when the prosecutors are confident that they have a watertight case against the former deputy president, will they announce the final list of charges.

During this period Zuma will be politically impotent and under immense personal strain. After all, the NPA is out to win and will be digging very deep to find the evidence it needs.

According to legal experts, the NPA is not allowed to use the court records of the Shaik case – and anything the judge said during that trial is inadmissible. So my guess is that the NPA will be opening many new cans of worms during the next few months, and other unhealthy relationships may well emerge.

Apart from providing some amusement value and helping us sell newspapers, what possible good can Zuma's trial serve?

The loony triumvirate of the ANC Youth League, Cosatu and the South African Communist Party clearly believes that Zuma has a better-than-sporting chance of clearing his name and returning to high political office.

One of the things I discovered during my days in the bond market was how to cut a bad position. Never fall in love with a portfolio of underperforming investments in the hope that things will get better. Sell them, take the knock and concentrate on a new strategy. The loony triumvirate has much to learn.

However, let's hypothesise and assume that Zuma is found innocent. That would also imply that Shaik is not guilty of having had a corrupt relationship with the then deputy president. Would Zuma expect the slate to be wiped clean and to be returned to power immediately? Would the ANC obligingly remove the incumbent deputy president and reopen the front bench to him? Would there be no hard feelings? I don't think so, somehow.

The trial of a deputy president is not an amusing sideshow; it's an unwelcome focus on the less savoury aspects of our new democracy. It has the potential to be politically explosive and, even if Zuma is convicted, it will still be a Pyrrhic victory. The best thing for South Africa would have been for Zuma and the loony triumvirate to accept the findings of Judge Hilary Squires and for Zuma to accept his political destiny and be allowed to fade quietly into well-deserved oblivion.

Cosatu strikes out on basic economics

3 July 2005

On Monday South Africans were treated to the odd spectacle of people fortunate enough to have jobs going on strike as a protest against unemployment. Clearly the irony was lost on most of those who took to the streets. I dare say if their union leaders asked them to paint their buttocks bright green and amputate their little fingers most would do so unquestioningly.

Cosatu evidently believes that jobs are conjured up at whim by politicians and big business, and similarly made to disappear. For example, the decision to retrench mineworkers, as far as Cosatu is concerned, has nothing to do with the viability or profitability of a mine and is an act of pure malice. Similarly, the textile industry could easily afford to employ more workers. All it has to do is ask the government to make it a criminal offence for South Africans to buy cheap foreign imports. Admittedly, the price of clothing would rise dramatically, but that shock to the wallet would surely be worth the cost of subsidising inefficiency.

That, after all, is really what Cosatu's strike was all about. It wants the government to remove all international competition from the market. It's so unfair that Chinese textile workers, who sew away for a dollar a day, should be allowed to sell their well-made, cheap garments to bargain-hungry South Africans. So the obvious answer is to ban all cheap imports and force South Africans to pay higher prices.

But it's not only cheap foreign imports and a strong rand that Cosatu objects to. It also wants local authorities to stop privatising basic services because, it believes, this will result in job losses. It is absolutely right, of course, but the idea is that privatisation will also result in greater efficiency, and that's not a concept Cosatu really understands. Companies are not supposed to be profitable or efficient; they are supposed to create jobs and give annual wage increases above the rate of inflation.

Cosatu's woolly thinking on unemployment is based on the notion that a job is a basic human right, which it isn't. If you are fortunate enough to have a job, it is because someone believes that you have skills, mental or physical, that are worth paying for.

Unfortunately, there are no guarantees that any job is for life. Victorian gas-lamp lighters were made redundant when electric lights were introduced in London and the rise of the newspaper industry wasn't good news for town criers. Robots have replaced humans on car production lines and if you phone a company to ask about its products the chances are you will be talking to somebody in India. It's all to do with the cost of operation, and the lower the operating costs, the better chance a company has of gaining market share and increasing profits.

What does it do with the profits? Well, if Cosatu had its way the profits would be used to pay the wages on unnecessary new jobs. Then the company would quickly cease to be competitive and, eventually, every job would be lost.

There's nothing sinister about the wide disparity between workers' wages and management salaries. It's simply a matter of saleable skills.

If I were employed as a low-skilled worker in a country with as high an unemployment rate as South Africa, I certainly wouldn't be heeding Cosatu's call to strike.

Hog heaven for a teenage hyena

10 July 2005

I'm not sure if this ritual still exists, but when I was about to finish school I had to spend an hour with Mr Robinson, the careers master. As with most things at a boy's boarding school, this was compulsory.

Mr Robinson also happened to be my English teacher, so he knew me pretty well – or so I thought. His role was to assess my strengths and weaknesses, and steer me towards the right course at university and on to a fulfilling career which I would find rewarding both spiritually and materially; all part of the after-sales service of an English public school.

Bearing in mind he had to do this every year for about 80 boys, it was inevitable that he would have some spectacular failures.

Very few 17 year olds have much idea about what they want to do with their lives, and I was no different.

Mr Robinson's gambit was to ask us all if we had any particular career in mind. If we did, and he approved, he would nod enthusiastically and the hour's allotted interview would be over in about five minutes.

I told Mr Robinson that I wanted to grow my hair long and become a drummer in a rock band. Actually, I would have preferred to have been the lead guitarist, but I could never master the art of 'bridging'.

This didn't go down well with Mr Robinson, who felt that I ought to have a back-up plan for a career that didn't involve throwing televisions out of hotel rooms and participating in drug-fuelled orgies.

He ventured that I would be ideally suited, in his opinion, to a career as either a lawyer or a priest. At the time I had no idea that lawyers and priests often lead far more interesting lives than rock musicians. I dismissed the priest suggestion on the basis that Anglicans never get to become pope and asked him to give me a few other pointers as an alternative to law.

Fortunately, I had been useless at maths and science at school, so that ruled out a career as an astronaut, research chemist or accountant and made things much easier for Mr Robinson. We jointly explored the possibilities of teaching, publishing, estate agency, urban planning and joining the police force, but none of them had quite the same pull as being a drummer in a rock band.

One thing Mr Robinson never mentioned as a career opportunity was the possibility of becoming a tow-truck driver.

If there are still such things as careers masters I do hope they include this intriguing career choice in the smorgasbord of opportunity they offer our young people.

Given my time again, I would have even ditched the rock musician dream to become a hyena of the highways. Think of it: hours and hours of sitting in the sun reading the works of Shakespeare with the short-wave radio crackling away in the background, followed by a hair-raising dash to the scene of an accident with all that lovely twisted metal and gore. This is rubber-necker's heaven.

Then a good scrap with rival drivers and the satisfaction of hauling away the twisted remains of someone's new BMW and releasing it only when a hefty ransom has been paid.

More new cars on our roads means more collisions, which means more work for tow-truck drivers. This is one of the new growth industries in South Africa.

I wonder who rushes to the scene of an accident when two tow-truck drivers collide ...

Parenting stripped to bare essentials

17 July 2005

A couple in Nashville, Tennessee, were sentenced to two years' probation and ordered to take parenting classes after pleading guilty to hiring a stripper for their son's 16th birthday.

Down in the Deep South of the US, where family values are evidently still held in high regard, this offence is known as 'contributing to the delinquency of a minor'.

In her defence, the mother claimed that they had to do something special for their son, whose name wasn't mentioned but is probably something like Billy Bob.

'We even had grandpa there,' she gushed, a trifle ill-advisedly. Knowing a bit more than I did yesterday about Tennessee law, it's surely only a matter of time before poor grandpa is up on a charge of fathering a conspirator to a delinquent minor.

My sympathies are with the parents on this one. Fortunately I don't have any children but friends who do tell me that among the greatest pressures of parenthood are children's parties. In the old days, the recipe for a good party for five- to seven-year-olds was simple. All you needed was a clown who tied balloons in animal shapes, followed by a table loaded with fizzy drinks, jelly and sweets. The really good parties ended in a food fight but sensible mothers covered everything in plastic sheeting beforehand.

When the time came to go home you were rubbed clean with a damp flannel and that was it.

Now, you have to arrive in the right car, with a present that isn't going to look cheap compared with everyone else's. The party-giver has to make sure the food is suitable for little Johnny's latest allergy and, at the end of the evening, goody bags are handed out. The social status of the parents is dependent on the bags' contents and I'm told that they sometimes eclipse the guests' presents in value. So when you slip iPods into the kiddies' goody bags you know that everyone will remember the party, but you also up the stakes. The next party-giver will have to drop in at least digital cameras to keep face.

It gets worse when they get older. A matric dance is now a hugely costly affair. The girls have to be flown to Cape Town to meet their dress designer and they'll obviously need a couple more visits for fittings. Meanwhile, the boys have to get the transport arrangements right. It's now very passé to turn up in a stretch limo, so the creative energy of a top advertising agency has to be applied to come up with something a little flashier. The new Rolls-Royce Phantom would work, as would the Bentley Continental Flying Spur, but the real gasps will be reserved for those who land in a helicopter or hot-air balloon.

Then there's the pre-party, the after-party and the after-after-party to think about. The matric dance itself is generally a rather sedate affair, with teachers keeping an eye on testosterone levels. It's at the after-parties that things get wilder, and the exclusive after-after-party where the wheels really come off.

That's when junior develops a taste for Famous Grouse 30-year-old and Cohiba cigars, both of which would be frowned upon by the legislators in Tennessee. I doubt things are much different for teenage birthday parties, which is why I think the idea of hiring a stripper has a lot of merit. Not only is it cheaper, but it saves coy parents the bother of having to explain the difference between the sexes to their sons.

Lies, damn lies and dollar millionaires

24 July 2005

If you can scrape together just over six and a half million rands, then feel happy, very happy. According to the 2005 World Wealth Report, you are one of South Africa's 37 000 dollar millionaires, which means you are a member of an elite 0.082% of the population. There were only 25 000 of us back in 2002, but our numbers have swollen, and the experts say that the current wave of wealth explosion looks set to keep growing. Soon we dollar millionaires could make up 1% of the population.

Now before you get too excited, consider this: a million dollars isn't what it used to be. It won't buy you much of a home in New York and if you convert your dollar-millionaire status to sterling you can expect to buy a terraced house next to a railway line in an unfashionable suburb of London. You won't even have enough money left over to buy a car and you certainly won't be frequenting fashionable West End restaurants where a designer beef burger can cost R600. You will have to holiday in boarding houses on the south coast of England for two weeks every year because you won't have enough spare cash for a foreign holiday.

A million of anything sounds like a lot to a journalist, but that's because most of us can't count beyond 10 000.

A departing co-president of investment firm Morgan Stanley has just been paid $32 million to 'pursue other interests'. If he'd stayed with the company he would have earned a measly $16 million a year for two years. So it obviously made sense to resign because he collects the $32 million and can probably earn a similar amount pursuing that other interest. Being a mere dollar millionaire would hold no attraction to someone like that.

A new Rolls-Royce Phantom is a magnificent car and absolutely ideal for a millionaire, but it costs around R4 million in South Africa. That's around two-thirds of your total net worth if you only just make it as a dollar millionaire. Buy the car and you only have two and a half million rands left to play with, which will get you an unrenovated house in Parkhurst. Suddenly being a dollar millionaire doesn't look such a big deal, does it?

The problem with these reports is that they sensationalise statistics. The number of dollar millionaires in South Africa may well have grown, but I doubt if there are many senior ANC politicians who don't make the list. Most black economic empowerment beneficiaries would scoff at the qualifying figure. They only start counting at R100 million, and even that's regarded as small money these days. You only get taken seriously as a BEE player if you have half a billion rands to play with.

So what the World Wealth report people need to do is to admit that a million dollars is actually monopoly money, and set their sights a little higher. After all, name me one Hollywood star who would consider appearing in a movie for a million bucks. Even sitcom actors can get paid $250 000 for a weekly episode. Is Larry King hanging in there because he hasn't made any retirement plans? I don't think so, and he certainly isn't pulling a mere million dollars a year.

However, the real concern should not be that qualifying as a member of the elite 0.082% of the population no longer means much. We should be far more concerned that more than 99% of the population are still a long way from becoming dollar millionaires.

Go beyond Mad Bob to help Zimbabwe

31 July 2005

One of the great mysteries of life is why diminutive F1 racing supremo Bernie Ecclestone insists on wearing what looks like roadkill on his head. It's not as if the fellow is hard up. On the contrary, he's one of the richest men in Britain and surely able to afford a decent wig.

Another of the other great mysteries of life is why nobody has managed to get the smirking face of Mad Bob Mugabe in their cross hairs. Perhaps Mad Bob keeps safe by employing a lot of decoys and body doubles, but if ever there was a slimy individual whose continued ascendancy beggars logic, then that person is Bob Mugabe. Not that one in any way wishes to denigrate the democratically elected leader of a neighbouring country, which is why I've tempered my language considerably and only refer to him as slimy.

Mad Bob managed to beg, borrow and steal enough aviation fuel to get to China where he intends waving the begging bowl around and asking for donations to the tune of R1billion, plus some fuel to get back home to his grateful people.

He's also asked South Africa to lend him $1 billion and it looks as though he might be in luck. Not surprisingly, this has caused much frothing from the chattering classes. The letters pages of the newspapers have been full of recommendations not to lend this scoundrel a cent of SA taxpayers' money and Douglas Gibson, the Democratic Alliance's foreign minister in waiting, commented that this was 'not the time for short-sighted gestures of solidarity'. I was even contacted by e-mail and asked to rally the troops and lend my support to a demonstration against any loans to Zimbabwe, something I have no intention of doing.

As you have probably gathered, I am no fan of Mugabe. In fact, I keep a celebratory bottle of France's finest in the fridge should breaking news announce his sudden demise. However, to not lend Zimbabwe money on the pretext that it will underpin a tyrannical regime makes very little sense to me.

And if you want $1 billion to disappear into thin air, you don't need to give it to Bob Mugabe. There are plenty of corrupt SA officials helping themselves to considerably more than that and I don't notice any tax revolt taking place.

It's quite possible that Bob will cash the cheque at his local building society, refuse to pay back the International Monetary Fund and put an order in for a couple of bullet proof Maybachs. But that's not really the point, is it? After all, we know he's a piece of slime and we wouldn't expect anything more from him. No, the reason we should be bailing the Zimbabwean government out is far more straightforward. We have, through our policy of quiet diplomacy and putting the telescope to our blind eye, let the Zimbabwean people down in the most spectacular way. We have been witness to some of the most brutal and inhumane acts and all we have done is mumble something about not wanting to interfere with another country's sovereignty. A bail-out of $1 billion may prop Mad Bob up for a few more months, but the gesture will be remembered by the Zimbabwean people long after Mugabe is dead and gone. And if we don't support the Zimbabwean people in their time of need and shield them against complete financial ruin, they will also remember us.

Everyone's Brad Pitt after a few drinks

7 August 2005

Who the hell are the Committee of Advertising Practice in the UK to declare that overweight, middle-aged, balding men are unattractive and should be used in drink advertisements instead of hunks? This may be bad news for George Clooney and Brad Pitt, but it's damn good news for short, paunchy, out-of-work thespians who have probably been waiting for such a tailor-made role to come their way for years.

In case you missed the story in last week's *Sunday Times*, the new Committee of Advertising Practice code says that 'links must not be made between alcohol and seduction, sexual activity or sexual success'. Which is why drinks companies will now be forced to hire unattractive actors if they want to advertise booze. This is obviously intended to cut down on the problem of binge drinking in the UK, the theory being that anyone who watches the advertisement will immediately associate alcohol with fat slobs. Men will forswear the demon drink for fear of winding up unattractive, and women will chuck the habit for fear of winding up in the sack with the sort of person portrayed in the new ads as a 'drinker'.

Apart from being hugely insensitive to fat, short, bald men who don't drink and consequently can't blame their physical hideousness on booze, this is just another example of how the nanny state of Tony (mine's a half, please) Blair is brainwashing Britain. Having already outlawed smoking and suggested that those who do smoke are just below child pornographers and lawyers on the 'nice to know' scale, the nannies have now moved to booze. The directive to use slobs is only the beginning of a much more complex initiative to portray anyone who even mentions a vodka martini as a hopeless, double-visioned, staggering drunk who shouldn't be entrusted with the keys to an Aston Martin DB5.

Unfortunately, the nannies have bitten off more than they can chew on this one. Britain is a proud drinking nation and nobody there drinks because they've seen an advert that portrays it as a sexy thing to do. They do it because they like the taste and the more they drink the sexier everyone becomes. So the whole point of using unattractive men in the ad is lost, because if you're drunk at home when you watch the ad he probably won't look too bad anyway.

Anyway, it can only be a matter of time before South Africa follows the example of the Poms and the health minister starts insisting that drinks advertising only uses middle-aged, unattractive men with crimson noses. I await the call.

Why stop at smoking and drinking though? Why not target car advertising as well. Take a look at the current spread of car ads and you'll notice that only youngish, good-looking people with fine teeth drive cars. Is this not as misleading as the drinks adverts? Aren't the motor companies linking the purchase of a particular car with seduction and sexual success? If they're going to insist on middle-aged, unattractive actors in drinks ads, then it's only fair that they insist on appropriate actors for car ads – boring people for boring cars, and don't try and fool us that driving a Nissan Almera or Toyota Camry makes us any less invisible to members of the opposite sex.

A Puppet Protector, with strings attached

14 August 2005

Look closely at Lawrence Mushwana's feet and hands and I'm sure you'll find small holes where the strings are threaded whenever his puppeteers need to use him. The Public Protector has come under fire recently for his findings on what has become known as the Oilgate scandal and, more particularly, his exoneration of state-owned PetroSA and his refusal to probe the allegedly dodgy dealings of a company called Imvume.

Not surprisingly, my media colleagues staged a synchronised volcanic eruption calling Mushwana's findings, among other things, a whitewash. The real question, though, is whether we should be in the least bit surprised that an office set up by government to investigate the affairs of government should fall so short of expectations. After all, the power elite has long realised the folly of setting up the Scorpions investigation unit and is busy thinking of a way in which it can be merged with the Bloemfontein traffic cops without anybody noticing. So it's hardly surprising that the role of Public Protector should be little more than an example of Orwellian doublethink and that Mushwana should turn out to be a human marshmallow.

Where we have all gone wrong is in blaming him for being a piece of political putty. What we should really be doing is calling for the abolition of the highly paid position of Public Protector because, as Mushwana has so ably demonstrated, the position is little more than a bad-taste joke played on the gullible electorate by a callously cynical government. The real public protectors are newspapers such as the *Mail & Guardian*, which has bravely fought against some really ugly political and corporate bullying to publish the unvarnished truth in this matter. Oilgate may be the *Mail & Guardian's* story, but other newspapers and radio stations have frequently exposed wrongdoing at high level and not allowed the stories to die.

Lawrence Marshmallow may be a patsy, but I'm sure he'll survive the opprobrium of the media and go on to greater things, no doubt making a personal fortune in some hastily constructed BEE deal in the process. To suggest that Mushwana is lacking in vertebrae or that he deliberately chose to ignore salient features of the Imvume/PetroSA deal is to suggest that he didn't understand the role of the Public Protector. I submit that he understood the role only too well and never had any intention of doing anything other than serving his political masters.

I re-read George Orwell's classic *Nineteen Eighty-Four* last weekend. There are some scary parallels with South Africa 2005.

Does this paragraph ring any bells? 'The Lottery, with its weekly payout of enormous prizes, was the one public event to which the proles paid serious attention ... it was their delight, their folly, their anodyne, their intellectual stimulant ... the prizes were largely imaginary. Only small sums were actually paid out, the winners of the big prizes being non-existent persons.'

How many lucky winners have you ever read about on the front page of the *Sunday Times* since the lottery began?

So we've been duped by the dream of untold wealth and sold the ANC's version of newspeak in the shape of the Public Protector. As Orwell said, 'Ignorance is strength'.

How golf became the President's bogey

21 August 2005

Do you remember those photographs of President Mbeki playing golf back in November 2002? In case you don't, allow me to jog your memory.

The presidential spin doctors, concerned that their charge should be seen as a man of the people and not some cyber-surfing, nerdy intellectual with a leaky ballpoint in his top pocket, summoned the South African press to Pretoria one fine morning to watch President Tiger Mbeki, resplendent in golf shirt and all the paraphernalia, play a few shots. His personal pro, Craig Martin, beamed proudly at his new protégé and we were assured that the President would even be able to practise on his very own nine-hole golf course at his official residence.

Whiteys breathed a collective sigh of relief and reasoned that the President couldn't be all bad if he played golf. I commented at the time in this column that, if Mad Bob had been as smart and told everyone he was seizing white-owned farms for golf-course development, there wouldn't have been nearly as much fuss.

Well, as the poet Burns observed, the best-laid plans of mice and spin doctors gang aft a-gley and it appears that our President is not quite so enamoured with golf as he was back in 2002. Maybe he found out that he had no talent for the game. It is a notoriously frustrating sport and a really bad round can put you right off the idea of hitting a small ball around the countryside with a collection of bent metal rods.

I doubt President Mbeki has had much time to practise, even with a nine-hole course at his disposal. He has been so busy travelling around the world, brokering peace deals and meeting fascinating people, that he would have had little opportunity for golf. Or maybe his spin doctors have changed their emphasis and now think that the President is too honky-friendly and needs to appeal more to his traditional constituency.

Whatever the real reason, the President has come down heavily on golf-course developments, saying that they, along with gated communities, perpetuate apartheid settlement patterns. Golfing estates like Dainfern offer residents the illusion of normality, provided they never venture out of the confines of the estate. But not very far away, on the other side of those high security walls, there exists a vast informal settlement full of people seething with discontent.

It's too late now but the obvious solution would have been to develop a golf course where the informal settlement now is and drive the shack-dwellers even further away.

As anyone with half a brain cell knows, the only way to preserve land in perpetuity for the white man and his approved black chums is to develop a golf course. Just as black economic empowerment is a peaceful version of the sort of redistribution of wealth threatened by bloody revolution, so is golf-course development a peaceful alternative to the battle for land.

To use a chess analogy, it's a bit like castling to protect your king. Once you've built a golf course, the land in question is out of play and only the super-rich can afford it.

Divide the number of golfing estates among the number of genuine golfers and it's perfectly obvious that there is a massive oversupply of golf estates, which lends substance to my view that this is just a cunning way of hanging onto land and ensuring a plentiful supply of water at the expense of those who really do need it.

Please! Screen people who go to the movies

28 August 2005

One of my many vices is to sneak off to the cinema for the 9.45am show instead of sitting in the *Sunday Times* offices pretending to work.

I generally have the theatre to myself, although on the odd occasion I have had to share it with a few pensioners. It's rather like a private screening, which for R14 isn't a bad deal at all. I can sit where I want, talk loudly to myself, throw popcorn and belch on my half-litre of Coke without upsetting anyone.

Obviously the sheer decadence of frittering my time away watching a movie while more diligent men are building the economy of this country is a major attraction, but the real reason I choose to watch movies at these unfashionable times is that I have yet to meet a movie audience I like.

I went to a weekend showing of *The Hitchhiker's Guide to the Galaxy* recently, and three midgets sat directly in front of my wife and me. As the film progressed it turned out that these were not midgets but children of about 10 who had been dumped at the cinema while their parents did something more interesting. They all had cellphones and spent most of the movie either SMSing people or talking. They clearly had no interest in what was happening on the screen, so I kicked the back of one of their chairs very hard in the hope that they would think a murderous psycho-path was sitting behind them and shut up. My wife, who tends more to the Dr Spock school of child psychology, leaned forward and reasoned with them and they were quiet for at least two minutes before boredom overcame them again and they started to chatter.

It's well known that cinemas are going through a rough time and have had to offer special deals to encourage patrons back. My main reason for not visiting a cinema used to be that I didn't want to see any of the films on offer. Now I have a whole host of reasons for not wanting to go. I've got 90 channels of rubbish to sift through on DStv. By the time I've realised that there's nothing worth watching, the movie I might have wanted to see is already over. I've also got a tremendous home theatre setup with Dolby surround sound, which makes me want to borrow a DVD and watch it at home where I can also drink alcohol and smoke a cigar. Admittedly, there are many films which are much better on the big screen, but the trade-off doesn't make it worth visiting a real cinema. Chances are I'll be sitting in a glorified crèche with an audience of bored 10-year-olds waiting for mommy and daddy to finish their coke-snorting lunch and come and pick them up from the cinema.

Both Ster-Kinekor and Nu Metro are suffering, and I doubt whether their problems have anything to do with high ticket prices. The reason people like me stay away from the cinema is that it fails to deliver on our expectations. The cinemas may be spacious and comfortable, and the sound system may be state-of-the-art, but now ticket prices are so low, a two-hour movie is considerably cheaper than a baby-sitter, which is why parents are using them for that purpose. The road to prosperity and the way to win back audiences is to hike the price of movie tickets by at least 400% and attract the sort of people who actually want to see a film from beginning to end.

Oh, and if you could introduce a smoking and drinking theatre, that would be even better.

I'm prepared to suffer for my art

4 September 2005

Professor Anton Harber is the highly respected Caxton Professor of Journalism and Media Studies at Wits University.

These days his hair is not quite as wild as it was when he first breathed life into the *Mail & Guardian*, one of the most fearless newspapers in this country. Google his name on the Internet and you will find a cross-reference to Wits University's website where, unless I'm doing something wrong, the journalism or media studies faculty doesn't even feature. Has the prof lost his faculty?

Harber writes a regular, must-read column in *Business Day* and, just over a week ago, he wrote that Joburg needs a Gonzo journalist in the style of the late Hunter S Thompson.

Thompson blew what was left of his brains out earlier this year and his ashes were fired from a cannon in front of a select group of invited celebrities at his estate in Aspen, Colorado. The 'funeral' party reportedly cost $2.5 million, which is pretty impressive considering the host wasn't there to enjoy it.

For those of you who haven't read Thompson's short but seminal work, *Fear and Loathing in Las Vegas*, I think it can be safely said that, along with Tom Wolfe and Joan Didion, he was at the forefront of what became known as New Journalism, a largely autobiographical style of reportage which replaced objectivity with subjectivity and a hefty dose of hyperbole. Wolfe got very excited and stated that New Journalism 'would wipe out the novel as literature's main event', then went on to write a best-selling novel, *The Bonfire of the Vanities*, which neatly negated that theory.

Thompson was one of the more convincing exponents of New Journalism. The term 'gonzo journalism' was coined after the release of *Fear and Loathing* in 1972. Entertaining as it may be, there are two main problems with gonzo journalism. One is the almost complete absence of balance and fact, and the other is the copious quantities of alcohol and hallucinogenic drugs necessary to produce it. I rather doubt whether a collection of Thompson's meticulously kept investigative journalism notebooks will feature on any future Sotheby's auction list. The whole point of gonzo journalism is to get so out of your head that you are prepared to cover a story that no sober or sane journalist would dream of covering. Thompson did this with *Hell's Angels* when he infiltrated and wrote about them in 1966.

Explaining how it was done, he wrote: 'After 50 or 60 beers, we found a common ground, as it were.' Once you've got out of your head and covered the story, it's simply a matter of coming back down to earth and reconstructing what you can remember. If you've ever been really drunk you will know that, on the morning after, you can't even remember where your car is, where your wallet is, how many table dances you paid for or the name of the unfamiliar woman next to you in your bed. Apparently with drugs it's even worse.

Hunter S managed to pull it off for a while but eventually became a very ill and bitter man. Wolfe and Didion sold out to fame and fortune. If Harber really wants a 'Dr Gonzo' to portray cruel and crazy Joburg, then I'd be happy to oblige.

All he needs to do is persuade the *Sunday Times* to pay for my drinks and drugs and convince our company medical aid scheme that it was all in the interests of art.

Hitch your wagon to that soggy star

11 September 2005

Anything can happen between the writing of a column and its publication, particularly when, as is the case with this column, the copy
has to find its way to the printers a full four days before the newspaper
appears on the streets.

Those four days can make all the difference and should it already have
happened, then this column may lack a little impact. However, at the
time of writing, no Hollywood celebrities had cottoned on to the idea
of harnessing the aftermath of Hurricane Katrina to the rejuvenation
of their flagging careers. Even a few caustic anti-Republican comments
on prime-time TV can help a fading star get noticed, but first prize (the
Sir Robert Geldof Award for extreme caring) will obviously go to the celebrity who organises StormAid or whatever they decide to call it. In the
next few weeks I confidently predict that the celebrity rush to be associated with the sodden city of jazz will make the postdiluvian efforts of the
looters look like a watery stroll to the shops.

The most extraordinary thing about New Orleans is that all the major
television networks carried plenty of advance warning of the impending
disaster on their weather forecasts, and some even hauled in experts to
explain what would happen if the levees that protected the city of New
Orleans should fail. In fact, so much warning was given that the larger
TV networks managed to get their film crews to New Orleans and still
have enough time to scout around for the best camera positions long

before the hurricane struck. Only Noah had more warning, but he did have an impeccable source. So it does seem odd that it took the US government as long as it did to muster the relief effort but, as has been mentioned already, no one of any great consequence lives in Louisiana. That certainly seemed to be the attitude of the world's most powerful nation until it realised that the rest of the world was sniggering at its apparent inability to sort out a disaster in its own backyard.

Now the military relief effort is well under way, and that's the cue for Tinseltown to come to the party. It can be only a matter of time before the absurdly named Paris Hilton (that's a bit like calling your daughter Bethlehem Protea or Randburg City Lodge) hires a private jet and flies down with her entourage to lend encouragement to the rescuers. If someone can find a luxurious enough yacht for this publicity-hungry bimbo, then I dare say she could garner some extra limelight by rescuing a few people herself; although I doubt whether she would want too much to do with many of the inhabitants of the Big Easy.

Ben Affleck hasn't been doing too well at the box office lately, so it's a racing certainty that he, too, will make a low-key appearance in New Orleans, surrounded by news cameras and paparazzi. Then it will be open season, although B-grade movie actors will have to wait their turn. Let's hope the TV cameras are still there for them. Who knows, maybe someone will write a new blues song commemorating Hurricane Katrina. The blues, after all, is supposed to spring from human despair, and things don't get much more desperate than New Orleans at the moment.

So pray that the celebs stay away, because the people have enough problems already.

And on the seventh day ...
the banks opened

18 September 2005

Once the South African government had checked my chest X-rays and satisfied themselves that I wasn't black or a communist (or, worse still, both) they gave me the thumbs-up to enter the country as a permanent resident. That was back in 1981, and my first few days in the country were spent in the Rand Hotel in Johannesburg while I looked around for somewhere to live.

I remember wandering the streets of Johannesburg on Saturday morning and then going back to my hotel for a couple of beers and lunch.

When I came out of the hotel just after two o'clock, the centre of Johannesburg looked as though it was under curfew. The shops were closed, the streets deserted. Sheets of newspaper were whipped up by the wind. I went back into the hotel and asked what had happened, to be told by a desk clerk that South Africa closes at lunchtime on a Saturday and reopens for business again on Monday morning.

The suburbs weren't much better. You couldn't go to a film on Sunday and, although shopping centres weren't locked up, the shops weren't open, so all you could do was window-shop. If you wanted a beer on a Sunday you had to have a meal to accompany it and you certainly weren't allowed to sit outside on a pavement eating and drinking in public. Even petrol had to be signed for, although most pump jockeys either couldn't read or never checked the signature or they would have wondered why Ronald Reagan was buying so much petrol in Machadadorp every other weekend.

The godless suburb of Hillbrow was the only place you could flout religious convention and buy books and records on a Sunday, and I spent many a happy hour in Hillbrow Records waiting for Monday morning to come around.

There's something to be said for the yawning chasm between the shops closing on Saturday and reopening on Monday. In much of Europe, Sunday is still regarded as a day of rest and families devote the day to wholesome activities such as cycling along towpaths, having family lunches and building model aircraft. They don't have a choice because shopping isn't an option.

Even if you aren't particularly religious, there is something rather comforting about hearing church bells on a Sunday and being part of a slightly slower pace of life, even if it is just for day.

Sunday ceased to exist in South Africa long ago and, while I own up to occasional Sunday shopping, I probably wouldn't be too bothered if the shops were closed. If you can't get your life into some sort of order and buy fresh milk and bread on one of the other six days of the week, then you're probably dysfunctional.

Thanks to pressure from big business, Sundays have become just another day of the week, barely discernible from the others. Even if you like the idea of a day of rest, you're unlikely to get it because most of your fellow citizens feel under pressure to go shopping or to sit outside trendy restaurants, inhaling exhaust fumes and sipping overpriced cappuccino.

Now the moneylenders want to come into the temple. Absa, the shameless descendant of Calvinist Volkskas Bank, plans to open certain branches on the Sabbath. Given the fact that everyone else is merrily transacting, I don't suppose there will be any objections, but if you do get hit by a thunderbolt while you're waiting in the express teller queue, don't say I didn't warn you.

Splashing out by the shores of Poo Lake

25 September 2005

Hartbeespoort Dam (or 'Poo Lake' as it's now affectionately known) is one of the more popular leisure destinations in Gauteng, and for good reason.

Unlike Durban, Cape Town and Port Elizabeth, Johannesburg sits on high ground and has no natural water feature on which we can float our boats. Which is why Hartbeespoort Dam has gradually become the aquatic playground of the rich and famous of Gauteng. Completed as long ago as 1923, the principal purpose of the dam was to provide irrigation for the surrounding farmland, but then the developers smelt money and moved in.

Today the shores of Poo Lake are cluttered with eyesore developments: convoys of construction lorries rumble along the surrounding roads holding up traffic and throwing up great clouds of dust. The upshot of all this is that Hartbeespoort Dam is no longer a very nice place to visit. Greed, an apparent absence of any building regulations, and a generous dose of bad taste have transformed what was once a tranquil weekend getaway into a thriving residential node complete with faux Tuscan residences.

In winter the water level of the dam can fall dramatically and, back in the drought of the '80s, thick, green, rank-smelling weed lined the shores and had to be expensively removed. Low water levels and recurrent weed problems are natural hazards, though, and little can be done to prevent them. The real problem is the dam's unnatural hazard which is overpopulation and the more buildings that pop up, the lower the quality of life will become.

In the days when just a few developments lined the shores, it was possible to go out on a boat and find your own piece of tranquil water. That has already changed and it won't be too long before the dam is the watery equivalent of our congested roads. Obviously, anyone buying property there for a few million rands expects to have access to the water. If luxury car sales are anything to go by, the preference will be for big flashy boats. So expect the dam to be full of expensive floating gin palaces with names such as 'Far Call' (the obvious answer to the question, 'how much did it cost?') with ghastly men in rollneck sweaters and nautical caps swaggering around calling one another Cap'n. The mega-rich will obviously need to differentiate themselves from the run-of-the-mill fairly well off and will have helicopters on the back of their craft and their own personal submarines to allow them to explore below the surface and check whether the local municipality is telling the truth when it says that untreated sewage is no longer being pumped into the dam.

The great advantage of Hartbeespoort Dam, of course, is that there is absolutely nowhere to go – which is great news, because it will discourage boat-jacking. Once you've covered the roughly 20km² of the dam (considerably less if the water level drops), you've experienced everything it has to offer. There are no massive waves or squalls to cope with, and the chances of being overturned by a breaching whale are virtually nil. So it can only be a matter of time before the hawkers move in and a man bobbing around on a rubber dinghy offers you white coat hangers, sunglasses and DVDs of *Pirates of the Caribbean*.

Let the poor spend the off-season in Clifton

2 October 2005

Housing Minister Lindiwe Sisulu seems to have pulled the bunny out of the hat by persuading developers that big-ticket housing developments such as golf estates will, in future, only get building permission if there is a low-income housing component attached. In other words, anyone paying for the luxury bits will be subsidising the poor bits.

This is a marvellous idea in theory, but will it work, I wonder? For example, if you're about to shell out upwards of R5 million (which seems to be the going price) for a house on a designer golf estate, you are presumably hoping to buy exclusivity.

If Minister Sisulu's plans go ahead, then this will no longer be possible. As you watch your five-bedroom Tuscan mansion with views of the 12th fairway progress from foundations to finishing touches, you will also be able to watch the building progress of the rather more modest two-bedroom home of your close neighbour.

In the past, the low-income home would have been conveniently out of sight and at a safe enough distance for the sounds of kwaito to be lost on the winds. The whole point of the new dispensation, however, is that rich and poor live happily together in one community. The old idea of dumping the poor in the middle of the veld and expecting them to commute long distances to work is no longer an option.

The minister hasn't announced which luxury development will be pioneering this experiment in social engineering, but I read that 47 bodies and companies involved in the building industry have signed the agreement, so we must presume that it's all systems go. If it works well here, perhaps we can sell the idea to the US and persuade them to build low-cost housing for the displaced of New Orleans in Martha's Vineyard and the Hamptons.

Naturally, it will take a little time for rich South Africans to get used to the idea of having poor people living so close to them, but I'm told that the smell of boiling cabbage can be quite appetising and that you eventually become accustomed to the township sounds of the night. Anyway, look on the bright side; you'll never want for a caddy or a gardener.

Another long overdue idea to alleviate the chronic shortage of decent housing is the compulsory requisitioning of holiday homes. Take, for example, somewhere like St Francis Bay, where large, comfortable second homes stand empty for 10 months of the year while the poor people of the Eastern Cape live in the most appalling conditions. How can we call ourselves a caring society when houses stand empty while people are homeless?

The obvious solution is for the government to offer owners a small financial contribution in exchange for the use of their properties during the months they don't actually use them. Obviously at holiday time the poor would have to move out so the owners could come down and enjoy themselves, but 10 months in a decent home is better than nothing.

The same goes for all those empty apartments on Clifton's beaches. After all, it's surely only a matter of time before the poor buggers living in shacks next to the runway at Cape Town International realise that there's masses of vacant housing with running water and fine ocean views to be had just around the mountain, and decide to do something about it without waiting for Minister Sisulu.

Not for me the dubious joys of going car-free

9 October 2005

I have decided to boycott national Car-Free Day on 20 October on the grounds that it is an infringement of my personal liberty and bad for the SA economy.

People will arrive late for work (if they arrive at all), the cops won't be able to fine as many motorists for minor violations and the poor oil companies will lose a whole day's consumption just so our emphysematous planet can briefly catch its breath before we start pumping noxious fumes into the air again the day after.

Either we become a totally car-free society and go back to ox wagons or we accept that the car is here to stay and build more roads for them. The fact that our abysmal public transport system is unlikely to be able to take me anywhere I want to go is beside the point. Even if we had a state-of-the-art transport system I would still choose to travel by car for a number of reasons, the most obvious one being convenience.

I can get in my car and drive to my destination at a time that suits me. I can choose the scenic route and even stop off for doughnuts and coffee. I am cocooned in a luxurious leather-and-wood cockpit with my choice of music, and if I want to sing along I don't have to worry about disturbing fellow passengers. I'm not bothered about missing the last bus home and, most important, I don't run the risk of having some nutter packed with explosives sitting next to me.

Public transport is one of the great social levellers of the US and Europe, of course, and while I admit to using buses and trains when I am overseas, I can't pretend I enjoy it. Get onto a bus or into a subway carriage and you are forced to accept what cruel fate throws at you: some grubby old man who stinks of urine mumbling to himself in the corner, a loud crowd of youths with strange tattoos and body piercings, and Scandinavian tourists with gigantic backpacks that press into your face every time they turn around.

Even the average commuter is a sorry sight to behold with his dog-eared paperback, frayed shirt collar and scuffed shoes. Then there's the enforced proximity to people who may not share my fastidious views on personal hygiene. It really is a gross experience and it's hardly surprising that most of us would prefer to travel with people we know in the comfort of our own cars. Or, better still, alone.

Not content with suggesting that we leave our cars in our garages on 20 October and find alternative ways to get around, the government seems hell-bent on penalising those of us who either choose to travel alone or are forced to do so. How does it propose to do this, I wonder? If you buy a seven-seater Renault Grand Scenic and have only three people in the vehicle, will they fine you for four empty seats?

Am I seriously expected to have a passenger at all times in my sporty two-seater, or will a Maltese poodle do?

The government seems quite happy to get its hands on the many taxes generated by motor ownership, so how dare it allow us to go into debt to pay off an expensive car and then tell us we can't use it as we wish? The only way to get motorists out of their cars is to offer a public transport system that is faster, safer and much cheaper. Since the chances of that are about a zillion to one against, I suggest you join me and give the finger to Car-Free Day on 20 October.

One final illusion from the Amazing Kebble

16 October 2005

The funeral of the infamous nocturnal aviator, Brett Kebble, brought to mind scenes from a Francis Ford Coppola film – the ones of a Mafia funeral with long shots of men in absurd clothing (announcing to all the world that they are gangsters) paying their final respects.

Kebble's high-profile mourners didn't disappoint. They called him a great South African, a visionary, a man who truly understood the principles of black economic empowerment, and a generous benefactor to the arts and various charities. Some even went to the trouble of wearing dark glasses to add the necessary touch. The only people missing from the funeral were grateful shareholders telling us how well Kebble's stewardship of various companies had done for their pension plans.

Whatever else Brett Kebble may have been (gifted mimic, piano player, driver of fast cars, amusing raconteur, loving husband and father), he certainly wasn't a great South African. He didn't, for example, start businesses and breathe life into them, thereby creating jobs. In fact, it's very difficult to work out how he acquired such great wealth and political influence without having to draw the inevitable conclusion that he was little more than a financial illusionist, the David Copperfield of the balance sheet. Copperfield could make the Great Wall of China disappear and reappear and Kebble could do the same with a company's assets.

If you really want to live the high life for a while, then see how many credit cards you can amass and use one to pay off the debts of the other. Put simply, this is what Kebble appears to have done on a grand scale. It's also very easy to be a generous benefactor when it isn't your money. So a couple of hundred thousand here and there to buy influence and keep a corrupt politician happy is no big deal in the greater scheme of things. Hardly surprising that there were so many sad faces at the funeral. Unless a new benefactor can be found it looks as though some officials of the ANC Youth League may actually have to find real jobs.

The small matter of an immense amount of money owed to the tax-man also negates any claim that Kebble was a great South African. Surely great South Africans pay their green fees and settle the bar bill when the account is presented? I suppose it's possible that the violence of Kebble's death caused some over-emotional senior politicians to say things they didn't really mean, but it's unlikely. What the Kebble funeral did was to send a clear signal to law-abiding, tax-paying citizens that they are regarded by those in power as insignificant jerks. As Gordon Gekko said in the movie *Wall Street*, either you're an insider or you're an outsider.

While the qualifications to become an insider may be unsavoury, we are left in no doubt as to the sort of economic activity the ANC prefers; one that produces upfront, risk-free cash benefits for those in a position to pull strings.

Finally, I used to wonder whether Presidential Rottweiler Essop Pahad was naturally stupid or whether, like me, he had to get up every morning and practise. I now realise that he is not stupid at all; just very, very dangerous for democracy.

Writing's on the wall for wannabe landlords

23 October 2005

I read recently in a financial journal that 30% of bond loans granted are now for the purchases of properties to let.

I'm usually quite good at handing out sage financial advice but, regrettably, not quite so good at following it myself. I doubt whether it will be any different this time, but my gut feel tells me that now would be a great time to put my house on the market and move into rented accommodation for a couple of years.

The only problem with this is that property ownership is often an emotional rather than a purely financial consideration and, besides, the idea of having to pack 14 years of accumulated rubbish into a removal van really doesn't hold much appeal.

However, if it really is true that 30% of new loans are for the purchase of rentable properties then, like Belshazzar's Feast, the writing is most definitely on the wall.

I've already heard tales of woe from people who have managed to rent their 'investment' properties, but at a substantially lower rate than they hoped and well below their bond repayment levels.

That's fine if the housing boom continues and the capital gain in a year compensates for the loss of rental income, but this doesn't appear to be happening. According to the experts, the rise in property prices is slowing and a hike in interest rates next year could slow them down even more.

Caught up in the hype and excitement of a major property bull market, it is sometimes difficult to distinguish between fact and fiction. Can property prices really go up forever? Well, they haven't anywhere else in the world and a look at the New York, London, Hong Kong and Sydney property markets over the past decade or two will reveal that prices can go both up and down. Why should we be any different?

If you're long of property when the market falls and interest rates start rising then you can either sit things out and hope for better times or cut your losses and take a loss.

I've watched hideous townhouse and cluster developments pop up in the most extraordinary places and have often wondered who on earth was buying them. Since the majority of SA citizens can barely scratch a living it can only be the buy-to-let brigade. Besides, nobody in their right mind would be paying the sort of prices being asked to live next to a main road.

Unlike many European cities, we don't have an affluent migrant population who may be interested in renting accommodation. So there's a good chance that many of these properties will remain empty and unlet, particularly if they are situated in inconvenient areas. Why would anyone working in Sandton want to commute from Kya Sands? The oversupply of new property can mean only one thing: rentals will stay low or fall as investors scrabble to get some return on their investment.

Here's an even more interesting thought, though: if the government were to impose a huge tax on the ownership of unoccupied property and set off a wave of distress selling, they could almost certainly pick up property at below building cost and sort out most of the country's housing shortage from existing stock.

Car-Free Day's fatal flaw: too much parking

30 October 2005

The hug-the-planet muesli munchers came down heavily on me when I suggested giving the finger to Car-Free Day a few weeks ago. The following morning my e-mail inbox was brimming with messages marvelling at my insensitivity and wondering how I could live with the knowledge that I was handing over a polluted planet to my children.

That last one's easily dealt with; I don't have children and I'm not about to start apologising to my nephews and nieces for widening the hole in the ozone layer and hastening the demise of the riverine rabbit.

I had been booked to help launch a new car model on Car-Free Day, so I really couldn't avoid driving, but I doubt whether I would have made an attempt to leave my car at home even if that hadn't been the case. I did, however, calculate roughly how much it would have cost me to use public transport and taxis instead of my own car, and the findings were horrendous.

Assuming I had been prepared to get up at four in the morning, I could probably have just made my nine o'clock meeting in Pretoria, but I decided that wasn't really on. Local buses just don't seem to go where I need to go at a time convenient to me, so I'm forced to use taxis.

As I hope to live a few more years I decided to rule out the hell ride that is part of the minibus taxi experience, although watching a man steer an overloaded vehicle with a large spanner should appeal to my journalistic curiosity.

The alternative is a grubby old Toyota Cressida with the stuffing coming out of the upholstery and a driver who chain-smokes and complains about the state of the country under black rule.

The most comfortable choice would be to use one of the AA's smart new MetroCabs, which would have cost about the same but at least I wouldn't have had to listen to the embittered political ramblings of a washed-up white man.

Totting it all up, I reckon it would cost me at least R8 000 a month to leave my car at home.

Impressed as I was with the evangelical zeal of Radio 702's John Robbie, I decided that he was probably one of those kids who used to take an apple to school every day for teacher. Or maybe it was a potato.

I rarely did what I was told at school and my natural inclination is to disobey orders, particularly if they sound half-baked and come out of a politician's mouth.

However, Robbie did make the point that Car-Free Day had got us thinking about the topic, particularly when it became apparent that the whole political con trick had been a lamentable failure.

Why didn't I drive to work when I lived in London? Was it because public transport was infinitely more comfortable than a warm BMW on a winter's morning? No, the reason I didn't drive to work was that there was absolutely nowhere to park when I got there. This probably applies to most European cities and is the real key to why Car-Free Day failed here and will continue to bomb in years to come.

We use our cars with confidence in this country because there is always somewhere to park. If South Africans need to walk more than 200m to their ultimate destination after parking their cars, they prefer to stay at home. So, Jeff, if you want Car-Free Day to work next year, close all the car parks.

Appearing for the defence of Judge Hlophe

6 November 2005

The government's laudable attempt to get us to all love one another by passing laws forbidding us from making rude or insulting comments based on, among other things, race, don't seem to have made much impression on Cape Judge President John Hlophe.

I doubt if most of us would have ever heard of Judge Hlophe had he not apparently referred to a Cape Town attorney as 'a piece of white shit'. Since then his name has appeared in the papers virtually every day, and the long-running saga of racism within the judiciary looks set to bore us all to tears for months to come. For the record, it has to be said that Judge Hlophe denies the charge but, given the circumstances, he would, wouldn't he? Last week Judge Hlophe lectured attorneys on courtroom etiquette, told then how to dress correctly and warned them not to criticise judges' decisions in public.

Only a complete lack of interest in constitutional law and the close proximity of El Vino's in Fleet Street prevented me from becoming one of the greatest barristers in the history of English law. I even became a member of Middle Temple, where members traditionally have to eat a prescribed number of dinners each term. Since the wine cellar at Middle Temple was reputed to be the best of the four inns, this was no great hardship. I read my Smith & Hogan: Criminal Law with a voracious appetite and committed to memory some of the more obscure sex laws such as The Slander to Women Act, which makes it a criminal offence to publicly speculate about the sexual appetite of a woman. Sadly, though, the world of the wig and gown, musty chambers and briefs tied with pink ribbon was not for me. However, this short and expensive flirtation with the idea of a career at the bar admirably qualifies me to come down firmly on the side of the Cape Judge President in the case of The Media vs Judge Hlophe.

Firstly, let's deal with his comments on etiquette, dress code and the appalling American behaviour of lawyers leaping up in court unbidden. A courtroom is a serious place and, should I ever find myself in one, I really don't want to be prosecuted by a circus clown in a green jacket, a red Donald Duck tie and a pair of leather sandals. The prohibitive cost of dressing properly kept a lot of what we used to call 'the working classes' out of the English courtrooms, and I don't think it's a bad idea to apply the same rule here. Judges should send home attorneys whose dress sense offends them. Court etiquette has changed over the years; it's no longer appropriate to preface an insult with the words 'if your lordship pleases' or refer to the opposition through gritted teeth as 'm' learned friend'. That said, the habit of modern attorneys of announcing that they are going to appeal as soon as the guilty verdict is handed down makes a mockery of the court system. Why not just toss a coin for a result? The decision to appeal a judgment suggests either that the judge's grasp of the law is shaky, or that the judge is crooked and has been bought.

Finally, whether or not the Cape Judge President used the highly descriptive phrase 'piece of white shit' is irrelevant and has no bearing on racism within the judiciary. He could just have easily referred to another attorney as a 'piece of black shit'. The question is, would that have been racist? No further questions. Court adjourned.

A leisurely drive down the information superhighway

13 November 2005

I'm feeling particularly pleased with myself this week. I worked out how to send an e-mail from my laptop through a telephone line linked to a switchboard.

Normally you have to dial 0 to get a line on a switchboard but just adding an extra zero to the dial-up number for my server didn't work. So I had this hunch that if I put 0 followed by a full stop in front of the telephone number everything would be fine. And it was. Joy. Now I know how Nasa felt when they finally got Neil Armstrong to get his lines almost right on the moon back in 1969.

I'm told they had to do three takes before a version that made sense could be transmitted to earth. Armstrong apparently spent the whole journey home sulking and muttering about how if he'd wanted to be an actor he wouldn't have signed up for the space programme.

A few months ago I discovered how to use predictive text on my cellphone. This is something anyone under the age of 25 is genetically programmed to know instinctively. When I first started out I would get halfway through a word that turned out to be gibberish and give up. Then someone told me to persevere with the word and press the relevant buttons and, hey presto, the word of my choice would appear, or one very like it.

But rather like the dictionary facility on Microsoft Word, my cellphone is a bit prudish and doesn't do rude words. Somehow 'dual off you aunt' doesn't quite convey the same level of hostility as the intended original.

Apart from creating a new language for communication and even spawning a new SMS-generation bible, predictive text can also be used for coming up with new names for places; something the more idle members of the ANC prefer to do as a substitute for real work. Thus Joburg becomes the rather attractive-sounding Locusi and Dainfern translates into the mystically named Echoedro.

Language purists tend to rant at the debasement of the English language but I can't understand why. All that's happened is conventional language has been stripped of unnecessary weight and fitted with a turbo booster. Think of it as the racing version. To me it demonstrates an economic ingenuity that is only possible if the creator of text language is fully in command of proper language.

It's already been shown that vowels are largely redundant and if I wrte a shrt sntnce in abbrvtd frm lk ths you cn gnrlly undrstnd wht I am tlkng abt. So the jump from a minimal use of vowels to the use of numerical symbols that sound like words or parts of words is a logical progression.

How difficult is to understand CU L8er, for example? It's a bit like the economy of language you're forced to use if you want a six-character personalised number plate such as 4NIK8R (fornicator) or I8A4RE (I ate a Ferrari).

Rather than spend half the morning laboriously sending an SMS I can now, through a combination of predictive text and SMS short-hand, get the same task done in a matter of minutes. This obviously leaves me more time for the really important things in life such as reading books. The only problem is that all those long sentences and complete words send me to sleep.

Pity the bloated beneficiaries of BEE

20 November 2005

In Africa the only way to become fabulously wealthy used to be to declare yourself the president for life of some obscure, newly independent country and direct all the proceeds from the sales of mineral wealth to your Swiss bank account – while everyone else in the country scraped by on less than a dollar a day.

The snag with this apparently flawless system of making a fast buck was the ever-present danger of being bumped off by someone from a rival tribe with similar ambitions.

How times have changed and how the previously disadvantaged must be rubbing their hands with glee as they become the currently super-advantaged.

Suddenly all those years spent in exile and all the beastliness they had to endure from the Nats have paid off.

They couldn't have done better if they'd hired Ed Fagan. The spectacular amounts involved in a particularly juicy BEE deal are way in excess of anything a judge would have awarded as damages.

The Europeans get very sniffy about African leaders who plunder their country's coffers while the majority of the people live in abject poverty, but BEE proves that if you plunder with panache you can get away with it.

Admittedly we may have a few million people (OK, quite a few million) who live in rat-infested shacks and haven't a clue what they're going to eat from day to day but that's only because they haven't taken the trouble to form an empowerment syndicate.

Pictures of the bloated faces of men new to the pleasures of over-indulgence stare out at us from the pages of the business press every day. Their taut skins seem barely capable of containing the bulging flesh beneath and their liverish eyes appear to float in an aqueous cocktail of Johnnie Blue and tears of disbelief. They have the look of men who know they have achieved greatness, even if they don't quite understand how it all happened.

Naturally such deals raise questions of political chicanery and crony capitalism, but surely it's all a matter of common sense.

If, for example, you are a democratically elected politician and have just acquired a personal stake worth R100 million at current market valuation in a public company, there are only two questions that need to be asked. Firstly, did you pay the R100 million out of your own pocket for that stake and, secondly, if you didn't, where the hell did you find a bank willing to lend you so much cash with so little collateral? If you didn't pay for the shares and have no obvious means to do so then the deal is obviously bogus and should be regarded as a kickback for political favours.

As a peaceful alternative to bloody revolution and the involuntary redistribution of wealth, I suppose BEE has some merit. It is, after all, the green fee that allows big business to continue playing while opening new political doors. The beneficiaries are a different matter, though. Instead of envying them we should pity them because their shortcomings are there for all to see.

They obviously lacked the guts, initiative, capital and brainpower to start their own businesses, which is presumably why they chose to become politicians and influence-peddlars. There is always something new out of Africa or is there?

The ugly wail of a fat cat in a hurry

27 November 2005

On a stretch of the N1 between Bloemfontein and Colesberg, a large white SUV drives up behind me, mid-afternoon with its headlights on.

Behind it I can see the flashing blue light of what I assume to be a police car. I am travelling at the legal limit but the SUV seems to be in a hurry. There is traffic coming from the opposite direction, but a short wait will soon allow the pursuing SUV to overtake. I wonder if I shouldn't pull into the emergency lane to let it pass, but remember the police car following. Even more shameful than being arrested for speeding would be pulling into the emergency lane to allow somebody else to speed and getting arrested for that. So I decide to carry on driving in the single lane provided and not risk a fine.

When the oncoming lorry has passed, the white SUV makes an exaggerated swerve to overtake, followed by the police car with flashing lights.

The police car sounds a honking siren and a cop on a cellphone in the passenger seat glares at me and wags his finger. I'm tempted to flick a V sign but know that if he stops me I'll be keen to punch his stupid face, so I ignore him and carry on listening to Sting on the CD player.

Put a half-wit in a uniform and give him a fast car, a flashing light and a siren, and you have a recipe for mayhem. We all saw it with Mad Bob in Zimbabwe. In the early days he enjoyed roaring through Harare with a phalanx of riders on powerful motorcycles, sirens at full volume – Bob Mugabe and the Wailers, as they were known. The motorcycle escort gradually diminished as the buffoons riding them failed to negotiate a corner or lost control on a slippery road. Bob's foreign exchange reserves didn't run to replacements, and outriders on bicycles are hardly befitting a mad dictator, so I believe he travels less conspicuously these days.

The lunatic on my tail on the N1 was, I suspect, one of our new fat cat provincial politicians with his very own bully-boy police escort. I guess he was dashing off to do something really essential like rename a dam or join an empowerment syndicate. No surprise in that. We know that most of our minor-league politicians are work-shy spivs with an eye on fast bucks. The real question is, what were the cops doing there? Haven't they got better things to do than break the speed limit on a major road pretending to escort some bigwig down a stretch of near-deserted highway? The answer is probably yes, but, when you pay the police as badly as we do in this country, it's hardly surprising that they'll leave their uniforms on and offer personal services for a few extra rands. If memory serves, the Thatcher boy tried the same trick when he lived in Constantia during his coup-hatching days.

The danger with this type of thing is the cockiness it engenders. The police car that overtook me with a honk of its siren knew that I had done nothing wrong. I wasn't speeding and I hadn't pulled into the emergency lane. What I possibly had done was slow down their paymaster. If we had stopped to exchange pleasantries I have no doubt that the Dogberry attitude of the cops could have caused me a lot of discomfort. It's very difficult trying to reason with somebody who barely made it to Standard 7. Which is why I suggest you always keep a couple of R100 notes tucked in your driving licence. Just in case you mislay your wallet, you understand …

Commuters ride the caboose on this one

4 December 2005

Let's get one thing straight about the controversial Gautrain project: it has nothing to do with coming up with an efficient transport system for Johannesburg.

If we wanted a more efficient transport system, we would be widening roads and adding bus lanes which, as has already been suggested by transport experts, is a much more intelligent allocation of scarce resources. The rail transport system (the part that hasn't been torched, that is) falls woefully short of even Third World standards and, bearing in mind the poor image of rail transport in Gauteng, it hardly seems worthwhile spending the money to improve the service.

While burning the already scarce supply of operational rolling stock may not appear to be a sensible way of improving an already lousy service, it does indicate the level of anger reached by the wretched souls who are forced to use these uncomfortable and unreliable cattle trucks to get to and from work every day.

My sympathies are with the commuters on this one. Years ago, when I used to commute to London on what was then British Rail, I frequently experienced similar pyromaniacal temptations when what should have been a 12-coach peak-hour train arrived with only 4 grubby coaches. The only reason I never set fire to the carriage was that it was always too damp to make a really good bonfire.

Those who commute by rail usually do so because there is no other way of getting to work. So, if the service they rely on regularly lets them down and leaves them stranded with no apology, it's hardly surprising when they lash out in frustration. A decent peak-time bus service would be a much better idea for a number of reasons. Not only is it a substantially cheaper form of transport, but it is also more versatile.

If a train breaks down, it blocks the track and every commuter in every carriage is affected. If a bus breaks down, fewer commuters are affected and it's a fairly simple task to bring another bus along and get people to their destinations. Unlike a train, a bus can take another route if the usual route becomes congested. Quite frankly, train versus bus is a no-brainer.

The proposed Gautrain will do nothing to alleviate the woes of current rail commuters. Neither will it tempt many people out of their cars, because the motorcar gives the commuter the freedom to decide when to travel. If we had Germanic railway efficiency in this country, then a timetable would mean something – but we don't.

Its construction will cause horrific traffic problems in already congested areas such as Sandton, not to mention the negative environmental impact it will have.

So, given the strong arguments for dumping this ludicrous boondoggle, one wonders why it's still on the agenda. One reason could be vanity. We don't have a showpiece commuter train and it would be nice to have one by the time all the footie fans arrive in 2010. No, that doesn't sound too convincing, does it? So the only possible reason for wanting the Gautrain is that its billowing cost (already up to R20billion from R7billion) is designed to line the pockets of all sorts of people along the way. Remember the arms deal?

Wake me up when this merry hell is over

11 December 2005

Sometime within the next week, I will have to crawl into the loft and drag down the fake pine Christmas tree in an attempt to be festive. There are at least three boxes of tinsel and things to hang on the tree, and the painted fir cones which hide the ugly plastic feet of the fake tree from view are at least 15 years old. Some of the tree decorations are considerably older.

The Christmas lights for the tree are put away carefully in their box every January, but somehow manage to tangle themselves during the year, so I know that they'll take at least an hour to unravel, and that the whole ghastly tree-dressing thing will take about an hour and a half if I am to get it absolutely right.

Absolutely right means doing the same, as near as possible, as last year and all the preceding years. The fake Christmas tree's appearance year after year is a symbol of family continuity. With its twinkling coloured lights, it's a reminder of past Christmases and a beacon of hope for the years to come.

What a lot of cobblers! All the Christmas tree's annual dusting down signifies is that another 12 months have sped by and all I have to show for it is unruly eyebrows, more lines on my face and still no invitation to join an economic empowerment syndicate as a token white benefici-ary. Maybe a stint on the next series of *The Apprentice* would help. That R100million for doing sod-all apart from handing over a couple of Cabinet ministers' private telephone numbers would come in quite handy. Particularly now the BMW M6 and the Aston Martin Vantage are available. In fact, I could buy both for cash and still bathe every day in vintage champagne on the interest generated by the balance.

As you may have gathered, I hate this time of year.

I can't stand the higher levels of inefficiency and incompetence which are automatically blamed on the festive season. I can't stand the way many Johannesburg restaurateurs assume we all have holiday homes at the coast and close up for two weeks, and I can't abide the fake jollity of all those bloody Christmas trees in the shopping malls. I don't like the stress of buying presents, because I never know what to buy, and I'm equally bad at telling people what I would like for Christmas.

Unless you pin them to the wall or hang them on a string, the Christmas cards blow down every time there is a gust of wind in the house. Not that we get many Christmas cards these days. I decided they were a dreadful waste of money years ago and now only send a few to very close friends, which is a bit pointless, because you're supposed to send them to people you hardly ever see. I still get cards from distant relatives and I can't even remember who they are or what they look like. I want to tell them to please remove me from their mailing list, but think it might be insensitive, so I don't send them cards and hope they'll take the hint.

I know I'm not alone, and that festive-season stress affects many people at this time of year. What we sufferers need is an exclusive resort (are you reading this, Sol Kerzner?) called the Humbug Club, where like-minded people could disappear between 6 December and 6 January and not be reminded of Christmas at all.

No paper hats, no Christmas pudding on the day and no Boney M ... just normality, and a gentle easing into the new year without all the fireworks.

Petrol industry needed to get the lead out

18 December 2005

What a wonderful time of year for a petrol shortage – and just as you were about to hitch up the Jurgens and set off for two weeks of sheer hell as well. Not that there is a petrol shortage ... well, not according to Lindiwe Hendricks, the minister of Minerals and Energy. It's just that it isn't reaching the petrol pumps.

Cynics may say that a Cabinet minister would be hardly likely to suffer from a fuel shortage because politicians look after themselves first. Besides, they have flunkeys to fill their expensive, taxpayer-sponsored vehicles for them and obviously wouldn't have a clue what happens at a petrol pump. This is the season of goodwill, though, and I refuse to entertain such an impure thought.

I prefer the view that the minister was forced to deny there was a shortage of petrol just in case those snooty Europeans get the impression that South Africa is a southern state of Zimbabwe. It's not that we can't afford petrol; it's just that we can't send it where it's needed.

I couldn't help wondering what all those foreign tourists thought when they flew into our world-class tourist destination of Cape Town last weekend and heard the pumps had all run dry – so they wouldn't be flying out again in a hurry. They probably weren't too impressed, but at least they could spend a candlelit night in the Mother City as the electricity failed yet again.

If you're a foreign tourist and reading this, take heart; the water is safe to drink and you can walk on our beautiful mountain providing you take an armed guard with you.

Not surprisingly, it wasn't long before the blame for the petrol shortage was dumped on the media. Apparently, people had been filling their tanks as soon as early rumours of empty filling stations became a confirmed news item. What a neurotic thing to do. Rather like all those people in New Orleans who stocked up on food and candles ahead of the hurricane.

The petrol industry then weighed in with the astonishing observation that motorists were panic buying their product. Prudently filling our tanks, I can accept – but panic-buying? I never saw people queuing with jerry cans to stockpile fuel – and topping up our cars with petrol is what the petrol industry surely wants us to do. Why else would they spend so much on advertising?

In the end, it all comes down to accountability. What the alleged petrol shortage demonstrates yet again is that South Africans don't like to be held accountable. Someone has screwed up, and blaming increased demand, panic-buying or the conversion to cleaner fuels is nothing more than a red herring designed to protect the incompetent nincompoops responsible.

Since the whole of South Africa closes for most of December and goes on holiday (as it has done for decades), one might have assumed that this could very possibly lead to an increased demand for fuel. Clearly this thought never occurred to the strategists in the industry.

Fortunately, Mr S Claus won't have to worry about such things next weekend when his sleigh arrives from Lapland. He converted to reindeer power years ago and they're even more economical to run than unleaded camels.

Gluttony and lust are resolutions
I can keep

4 January 2006

I dumped the idea of new year resolutions a couple of years ago and decided instead to devote the month of January to systematically committing the seven deadly sins in no particular order: much easier and considerably more enjoyable than trying to give up smoking or drinking for a month.

Gluttony, pride and lust were a doddle but envy proved a bit of a challenge. Who on earth is there left to envy? I got quite angry when I realised the best I could muster was a grudging admiration for Jeremy Clarkson's ability to con an Aston Martin DB9 out of the Ford Motor Company as a long-term loan car. But I'm not sure it counts as envy.

Anyway, I obviously score high on anger on this one and my lack of envious enthusiasm gives me an A for sloth.

Which leaves only avarice, which I'm much too busy to be bothered with. So five out of seven isn't bad and I get straight As in everything except envy and avarice, and a distinction in lust.

Which brings me back to new year resolutions. Consider for a moment the well-used phrase 'botched circumcision'. You normally hear it bandied about during initiation time when scores of male youngsters are painted white, given blankets to hide their nakedness and taken into the wilderness by a bunch of weird old codgers so that they may become real men.

Unless I've grabbed the wrong end of the stick this is not something a lot of adolescents look forward to with great enthusiasm.

Now the word 'botched' may be spot-on when describing a bad plumbing job or an attempt at retiling the bathroom, but it's hardly appropriate when describing a failed circumcision, particularly if you happen to own the penis that's on the receiving end of the botching. When I botch the tiling I can admit defeat and call in the experts, but the unfortunate survivor of a botched circumcision isn't quite so lucky.

Instead of passing to manhood, the poor victim is doomed to a life of pain, rejection and misery, thanks to the trembling hand of some old duffer whose fingers slipped or who forgot to use a sharp blade. This happens every year and there is always a public outcry and yet we are told not to interfere because it's part of our cultural heritage.

Painting my face blue is part of my cultural heritage, as is witch-burning, dwarf-tossing and fox-hunting. That doesn't necessarily make any of them a good thing, or particularly relevant to modern-day living. Times change and the old barbaric and superstitious practices eventually give way to new, less harmful, barbaric and superstitious practices such as reality TV.

Perhaps it's time South Africa came up with a new year's resolution to stop being so pitifully PC and admit that not everything to do with black culture is worth preserving. We are, after all, now on speaking terms with the First World and most of us have materialistic First World aspirations. Tales of secret initiation ceremonies and botched circumcisions seem strangely out of place in a society that is asking the world to take it seriously.

And while we're on the subject, maybe our disastrous health minister could be persuaded to jettison her medieval views on the cure for Aids.

Hoek of a foreign field that is forever Fransch

15 January 2006

Have you ever wondered what would happen to the Western Cape should this country go to war with France? Admittedly, the chance of a war with France is slight at the moment, but you never know; the tiniest things trigger hostilities and the one thing that could tempt the French to invade is the belief that Franschhoek belongs to them.

Having recently visited what was once a quiet, rural and very South African dorpie, I have to say that it would be an understandable mistake. Franschhoek is no longer quiet and rural. Large construction lorries rumble down the Grand Rue, which is decked out with French flags and other Francophile paraphernalia. In fact, when you enter Franschhoek you are left in no doubt that you are temporarily leaving the Republic of South Africa. Men with onions around their necks and striped matelot shirts pedal through the streets on black-framed bicycles, berets placed jauntily on the heads, a burnt-out Gauloise between their lips. Under the traffic cameras on the lamp posts they have fixed sophisticated machines which spray a fine mist of garlic and Chanel No.5 into the air. Impeccably dressed women sip exotic cocktails at roadside cafés while clutching miniature poodles, and wizened old men hum 'zank 'evans for leedle girls' as they play pétanque on the one strip of gravel that hasn't been sold for development by Pam Golding. In the market square stands the guillotine where criminals, and cattle rustlers from the neighbouring 'zone dangereuse', are beheaded in front of thousands of cheering villagers every week.

Actually, none of the above, starting from the words 'men with onions' would pass the rigorous *Sunday Times* accuracy test, but that doesn't really matter because it's probably only a matter of time before it all becomes true.

What started as a clever marketing plan many years ago has become an uncontrollable monster, with the result that Franschhoek is in danger of believing that it really is French. They even use French words to describe what the rest of us in this country call hotels or guest lodges.

Pretty soon the banks in the Grand Rue de Franschhoek will be putting up signs that say L'Absa or Premier National Banque, the convenience stores will rename themselves Le Spar and La Boutique Bienveillant and they'll start charging a toll for anyone not driving a Renault, Peugeot or Citroën.

What would happen, I wonder, if you wanted to open a Mongolian stir-fry restaurant in Franschhoek? Would you have to call it Maison Genghis?

You might think that an entire community of extremely wealthy people all running around pretending to be French is nothing more than harmless fun, even if it is a bit confusing for foreign tourists who think they're visiting South Africa. However, it's the thin end of the wedge and if the government of the Western Cape (I'm assuming they have one) doesn't intervene soon then other traditionally South African dorpies may also be tempted to buy up old national flags and play make-believe.

Grabouw could easily become German, complete with an oompah band, Elgin Greek and Pringle Bay Spanish. It's only when Khayelitsha thinks it's Palestinian that we'll really have a problem on our hands.

Anything but the licensing department

22 January 2006

Isn't it about time that we simply accepted the Christmas road death figures as one of the hazards of living in South Africa and stopped fussing about them when they exceed the previous year's?

After all, if you live in Hemel Hempstead in Hertfordshire, England, you run the risk of the local oil refinery exploding. If you live in Chernobyl your chicken Kiev really does glow when you turn the lights out and, if life really has dealt you a bad hand and you dwell on the banks of the River Ganges, then best you learn to swim.

Quite why dying on the roads at Christmas should be any worse than dying on the roads at any other time of the year I'm not sure. Perhaps the poignancy of unopened presents around the tree and an empty place at the Christmas table are supposed to scare us into driving carefully.

The official reasons given for the high death rate this year were speed and driver fatigue, but I would suggest that a lack of both intelligence and driving talent are equally to blame.

For example, if you squeeze 10 people into a car designed to carry 6 then you are asking for trouble. Most of us know that, but there's a huge percentage of the population who have managed to get anywhere near a car's steering wheel only in the last decade and, because of their lack of driving experience, they have a different understanding. They reckon that you can keep piling people or things into a car until the body scrapes the ground. That's why we have so many overloaded taxis on our roads.

Similarly, anyone not schooled in Newton's first law of motion will probably not fully comprehend that an object in motion tends to continue in motion in a straight line, unless acted upon by an outside force. Start talking about inertia and velocity and you'll be greeted by blank stares. Isn't that what the brakes are for?

The basic knowledge of physics that many of us take for granted is clearly lacking in a large number of road users, which is another reason so many cars veer out of control and finally make contact with an outside force. By then it's a bit late to be learning Newton's laws.

Most people really do think they can steer a car while talking on a cellphone, but the sad reality is that they can't. Neither, for that matter, can they control a vehicle while searching for a radio station, but that has never led to a call for the banning of radios in cars.

Speed is conveniently blamed for many accidents, but how can you expect South African motorists to travel at a maximum of 120km/h when pretty well every car sold is capable of far greater speeds than that? If the road ahead is clear, most of us apply a little more pressure to the right pedal and cruise quite happily and safely at illegal speeds.

So what's the solution? Perhaps the government should adopt a carrot-and-stick approach and allow those of us with powerful cars to drive them on certain stretches of road at any speed we like. The trade-off would be heavy fines and loss of our licence should we get caught speeding on regulated roads.

However, the greatest deterrent would be a requirement to retake a driving test if caught speeding or driving dangerously. The prospect of all that bureaucracy and queuing, not to mention the inconvenience of not being able to drive while we are applying for our licence, would make us all drive like Australians.

Aircraftiness: the art of covering up
a free ride

29 January 2006

I flew to London a couple of weeks ago with the chairman of one of the world's most prestigious motor companies. We were sitting in British Airways' Club class which, on the basis of four international flights in one week, I can proclaim is light years ahead of the competition when it comes to cheerful cabin staff and exceptional service.

I asked the chairman why he wasn't travelling first class and he told me that it would be a quite unnecessary expense.

How very different from our grasping politicians who have become the embarrassing adult version of the fat kid at the birthday party who pockets the chocolate cake he can't stuff into his mouth.

If anyone is entitled to travel first class it's the chairman of a successful, publicly owned company.

But what would be the point? Club class offers the comfort he requires and he has nothing to prove. Why burden the shareholder with extra cost just for an ego stroke?

That's where business and politics are so different. With politicians, the ethos is that if it's there for the taking then take it.

After the deputy president's ill-advised magical mystery tour to the UAE at taypayers' expense, the phrase 'gravy plane' came into common usage long before this column could lay claim to inventing it. Well, not to be outdone I give you: aircraftiness (n), using cunning and deceit to convince critics that you were crane-spotting and not just taking your mates on a free junket.

Another meaning of aircraftiness is to lay claim to an aircraft seat to which you have no entitlement. There are also the adjectives 'aircrafty' and 'aircraftily'. Typical usage might be as follows: 'Having been shown to his seat in the cramped economy-class section of the plane, the well-known television presenter aircraftily slipped into the one vacant seat at the back of the business-class section just after takeoff.'

Anyone in high public office who borrows an aircraft with no authority and no good reason and then invites some cronies along for the ride is either a) completely insensitive to public criticism, b) unaware of the rules, or c) a couple of sandwiches short of a picnic. No prizes for guessing which one I go for.

The talking toadies whose job it is to clear up after ministers really came a cropper on this one. Normally the lies flow easily from their lips, but on this occasion they had to keep reinventing new, and even more outrageous fibs to cover their earlier, ludicrous explanations. They evidently think we're all as stupid as they are.

Anyway, it's water under the bridge now and we must be prepared to forgive and forget. By now we should be so used to dodginess and corruption in high places that a R700 000 shopping spree should be seen as small fry.

Indeed, one of the ANC's many talking heads said as much, implying that we shouldn't worry our confused little heads about individual cases of corruption unless they go well into the seven figures.

My guess is that, having discovered the joys of a boarding pass-free world, the deputy president will be lobbying Parliament for her own private jet, painted in the ANC colours of envy green, unemployed black and kickback gold.

Mostly I gets my grammar dead right

5 February 2006

I was grinding coffee beans in readiness for my usual Sunday morning cappuccino when the child bride alerted me to yet another letter in the Lifestyle section complaining about my failure to grasp the basics of English grammar. Nancy Stratten had added her strident voice to the growing chorus of disapproval. Ms Stratten had earlier written to me pointing out that the use of 'you and I' was incorrect in the context of a column I wrote and that I should have used 'you and me'. However, it was Ms Stratten's plaintive, 'I wrote to him, chiding him gently. Sadly, he never replied' which spurred me to respond.

During the course of the week I receive many e-mails and letters and I apologise if, like Ms Stratten, you have written and not received the courtesy of a reply. Letters beginning with the words 'Dear Mr Bullard, we have produced an 18-year-old malt whisky and are thinking of releasing it to the general public once you have given it your personal seal of approval' receive an immediate response. All other communication is noted and usually receives a reply if one seems appropriate. Ms Stratten's gentle chiding did not receive a reply because I couldn't summon up the words to convey the gratitude I felt. What would have been appropriate, I wonder? 'Dear Nancy, thanks so much for the letter pointing out my grammatical deficiency. It bucked me up tremendously. By the way, you never mentioned whether you enjoyed the substance of the article. I can't blame the subeditors because it was my error and obviously slipped under their usually vigilant radar screen. Since we're on the subject of my fall from grace, I would like other offences to be taken into consideration. I was once slapped over the wrist for using 'hoard' instead of 'horde' (bloody subs again) and since reading *Eats, Shoots & Leaves* I've developed a form of Tourette's syndrome and now commit solecisms I never committed prior to reading that wretched book. Apart from an inability to walk on water, I have also been known to wear odd socks, dribble during long flights, leave the toilet seat up, hook third gear instead of first in a car and stare at women's breasts. I am, I confess, hopelessly human and subject to the same rules of fallibility as other carbon-based life forms of similar bodily shape. I wish I could say I won't do it again, but you and me know that is an impossible promise to make ...'

Hopefully this self-flagellation before the two million readers who devour this column every Sunday will make up for the lack of personal communication, Nancy, and, once again, please accept my humble apologies.

On a more positive note, the three grammatical errors above, while inexcusable and indicative of the decline of proper standards of English, represent less than half of 1% of my total output these past 12 years.

I'm sure there have been others that have been caught by the subeditors in their trawl net, but the published error rate reveals a 99.5% accuracy level if you exclude warped logic and dodgy opinions. So, if you read this column for the content you may well feel short-changed, but if you read it as an example of good English then you should be feeling very chuffed because a 0.5% margin of error really isn't that bad.

The first 100 years: what really happened

12 February 2006

Who could have failed to be moved at the wave of jubilation and national pride that swept our country last weekend on the occasion
of this newspaper's 100th birthday? In the great Basilica of St Peter the
Simple, the bells tolled without ceasing, a signal for all the church bells
throughout the land to join in the celebration. By sunrise long queues
had already formed and the Great Hall of the Heroes was filled with well-
wishers keen to pay their respects as they shuffled, heads bowed rever-
ently, past the imposing marble statues of the newspaper's past editors.

In the rural areas cows were slaughtered by simple peasant folk and
offered in thanks. In shopping malls a two-minute silence was observed
at midday. Even black economic empowerment beneficiaries took a few
moments from counting their money to reflect on this momentous occasion. In scenic Ogies, the production line at Flags t' Burn came to a
halt as day-shift workers observed the two-minute silence, despite the
production demands resulting from a large order for kerosene-soaked
Danish flags from the Middle East.

In the excitement of the moment it's easy to overlook the fact that
the newspaper celebrated its centenary exactly 20 years after the City of
Johannesburg's centennial. For two decades the people of Johannesburg
had nothing to read on a Sunday morning. No Prince Valiant, no Back
Page girl and no Gwen Gill column.

The great South African historian Professor Richard Brain believes that the 20-year wait for a 'Paper for the People' was largely due to the lack of a printing press.

Early settlers had arrived in the mid-17th century from Europe and, while they had remembered to bring vines and tulip bulbs with them, they had completely forgotten to bring a printing press. Or if they had brought one, they weren't lending it to the English.

Although small, insignificant publications existed in parts of South Africa, they were mostly written in neat calligraphy on vellum by teams of Tibetan monks.

Distribution was always a problem, and the slowness of the monk's writing generally meant that a story was stale by the time the ink was dry and the publication was circulated.

It was quicker to tell someone their village had been razed than to laboriously write it down and only break the news to them days later.

By 1904 the idea to start a newspaper to alleviate the terrible boredom of Sunday mornings had formed, and a printing press of sorts was fashioned from bits of disused mining equipment.

Over the next 18 months anyone wishing to seek his fortune in South Africa was asked to bring a few individual typesetting letters with him from Fleet Street and so, gradually, the would-be publishers amassed enough letters to produce a whole Sunday newspaper.

The churches pretended to be appalled but they secretly welcomed the *Sunday Times* because curates knew they could get away with shorter sermons now that people had other things to occupy their time on a Sunday morning.

Only those with dark secrets and something to hide rued the day the *Sunday Times* appeared; the same applies today, which is why our 100 years is well worth celebrating.

This year's best device is just a bit too good. Bring back built-in complexity, DStv

19 February 2006

Apart from the wheel, the iPod, pickled walnuts, the digital camera and mutton-flavoured chewing gum for dogs, the DStv personal video recorder (PVR) must rank as one of the most useful inventions ever.

Marginally larger than the normal DStv receiver, it allows the viewer to record up to 80 hours of programmes for future consumption. If the phone rings, you just press the pause button and the programme freezes and carries on at the press of a button later as if nothing had happened.

Obviously you can watch one channel while recording another and, if you're one of those affluent households with two TVs, you can watch two channels on different sets while recording a third programme. You can even set the machine to record the same programme at the same time every day or week for the rest of eternity.

Edging out both the espresso machine and the food processor, the PVR has just won the coveted 2006 Bullard Household Most Popular Appliance Award at a glittering ceremony held on Saturday in the kitchen just after lunch.

The great thing about the PVR is its simplicity of operation. No one reads instruction manuals, which is why none of us can operate our

VCRs properly. DStv knows this and so they've made their machine idiot-proof. Admittedly, it comes with a manual to make you feel as though you've achieved something, but the truth is you don't need a manual because even the child bride has mastered the PVR.

Utterly confused by the apparent complexity of her new cellphone, unable to drop the water level in the swimming pool without calling out a technician, and vague on the exact location of the bonnet-release catch in her car, she has nonetheless worked out that if you hit the red Rec button on the remote control, whatever it is you're watching on television at the time will be saved for repeated viewing.

And that's the problem. Apart from the collection of unwatched programmes that have already accumulated thanks to the time-based recording programme, we now have the Winter Olympics to contend with. Every time she sees anyone on a skate or a ski she presses the red button and we use up another 120 minutes recording the bump-skiing or the terminally dull cross-country. We already have at least seven hours of unwatched *Euromaxx* in German to get through, plus some *Top Gear Extras*, *Inspector Morse*, a programme about dolphins and several episodes of *The L Word*.

Now we're adding hours of skating, skiing and heaven knows what else involving snow and ice, and pretty soon that fairly generous allowance of 80 hours of recording time is going to be used up.

The simple answer would be to delete some redundant recordings to make way for new ones, but things are not that simple. Just as it's impossible for most people to not to answer a ringing telephone, so is it just as difficult to delete an unwatched recorded programme. We're going to use up 10 days of leave this year just watching our recorded programmes.

So, DStv, could you either give us an extra file disc with space for accumulated unwatched clutter (it doesn't actually have to play back because it probably won't need to) or, better still, could you make the controls on your next model a bit more complicated?

Let foreigners who pay for their place in the sun have their pound of SA land

26 February 2006

The debate over whether a moratorium should be placed on the sale of bits of South Africa to foreigners was bound to raise some hackles.

The loony Left regards anyone buying property in this country as a latter-day colonialist. This is the politics of envy and someone urgently needs to point out to these simple souls that real colonialists don't pay for land ... unless you consider the purchase of Manhattan from the Native Americans for strings of coloured beads payment.

At the other end of the political spectrum is the hard-nosed business point of view that warns that the threat of a moratorium will scare off investors and buyers' and tarnish South Africa's reputation in the world.

The idea of a moratorium on any future sales of land to foreigners has been mooted for a while and is perfectly reasonable, given this country's political situation. One of the essential ingredients for a good business environment is certainty and by formulating a clear policy for foreign land ownership the South African government would be creating certainty.

They may decide that there should be no further sales to foreigners, in which case the price of existing stock would probably be likely to fall dramatically, making property affordable once again for card-carrying South Africans. It may even find that all foreign ownership is abhorrent and give existing owners six months to sell their properties and go home.

That would certainly alleviate any problems the deputy president may have with the strength of the rand.

However, since those concerned with this delicate matter are reasonable, pragmatic people, I think it far more likely that a sensible and mutually beneficial solution will be reached.

One of the downsides with being a rapidly emerging market is the bargain-basement factor. Emerging nations, almost by definition, trade at a deep discount to emerged nations, which creates superb investment opportunities for those with stronger currencies. Property was an obvious case in point.

As little as five years ago you could buy a decent flat in Cape Town's city bowl for £40 000, an amount that could be put on a credit card. With a two-hour time difference from London, a convenient overnight flight and a lifestyle which matched the best of the more expensive Mediterranean resorts, it was a no-brainer. Even if the country went the same way as Zimbabwe, it was hardly a blow to the pocket of those property investors who decided to buy bolt holes in SA.

For years the property had been there for the taking and the only reason most South Africans didn't snap it up was that they were too busy working out what a small house in Perth would cost them. It was the foreign property buyers who taught us what the intrinsic value of our land was, and only after that did the locals climb on the bandwagon and push prices up into the stratosphere.

The ANC seems to espouse a free-market philosophy so they can't punish people for spotting a good opportunity in the early days and investing in South African property. But now membership of Club South Africa carries with it a greater commitment, and so it would be perfectly reasonable to charge foreign buyers a 25% premium on the price of the property and use that amount for much-needed social upliftment.

If they balk at that then we can always change the premium, but I don't think they will because you can still buy a magnificent Cape Town property for the price of a grim three-bedroom terraced house in Fulham and, even with no electricity, that's a bargain.

Take this, you Danish insufferable prigs

5 March 2006

So here we are, poised on the brink of global destruction, and it's all the fault of some obscure Danish cartoonist called Dov Zapirosen. Those newspapers unwise enough to have reproduced the cartoons soon wished they hadn't and the whole thing all became rather surreal.

It's worth remembering that you don't actually need to go to all the trouble and expense of finding a judge in chambers on a Saturday night to issue an interdict when a good old-fashioned death threat will suffice.

Clearly a mumbled apology isn't enough when you're dealing with a large body of deeply offended readers, and the only way to put things right is to give the Danes a taste of their own medicine by having a go at their Nordic gods. That should drag them away from their Lego castles and their Bang & Olufsens; although whether the Danes have it in them to go on the rampage is doubtful, bearing in mind young Hamlet's hopeless indecision over whether to kill his uncle for nicking the throne of Denmark from his dad.

I've already set the retaliatory ball in motion by daubing walls with offensive graffiti in the hope that someone from Denmark will see it, get really angry and reflect on the hurt they've caused others.

'Odin is raven mad' is one of mine, as is 'Thor wears a thong' and 'Valhalla is full of quiche eaters'. This is pretty incendiary stuff and we're publishing it only in the interests of press freedom. As a precaution, the lavish suite of offices from which this column is produced has been temporarily moved to a secret reinforced bunker.

The problem with giving the Danes a taste of their own medicine is that they have so many gods, goddesses, dwarves, giants, magic serpents, sacred trees and all the other paraphernalia of myth that it's quite difficult to know what's going to hurt them most. Since Odin is the king of the gods (self-appointed naturally) he's the obvious one to mock. Apart from riding the equine equivalent of a Harley-Davidson (an eight-hoofed horse), he also had some pretty odd ideas about marital fidelity and shagged just about everything from attractive young mortal women to geriatric immortal earth goddesses.

Add to this a paranoia beyond belief and you begin to get the impression that Odin bore more resemblance to a despot just north of our borders than a paid-up, card-carrying god.

He apparently had two ravens, Orkney and Snorkney (sorry, I'm a bit vague on the exact details), which he sent out to gather information every day. They would fly back and tell him there had been an earthquake in Chile or a train crash in Mumbai and update him on the rescue efforts. Not exactly news you can use if you're king of the Nordic gods.

Thanks to a quick snifter from the fountain of wisdom he also had only one eye, which made steering his eight-legged horse a bit difficult, particularly after he'd been carousing with the dead young men he'd taken off the battlefields and invited back to Valhalla for a few drinks ... very Dahmeresque!

So the king of the Nordic gods is a one-eyed, fornicating news junkie with a mid-life crisis and a penchant for dead men. But does he have a sense of humour?

Power to the people – but not from a plug

12 March 2006

I paid a fleeting visit to our very own dark land of Mordor, the Western Cape, last week.

I was there for a car launch, and of the 14 or so hours I spent at the hotel, about 9 were without electricity. That rather spoilt plans to hold the evening's event on the top floor of the hotel, with its spectacular sea views, and meant no coffee at breakfast, no light in the bathroom to shave by and a long walk down several flights of stairs with heavy luggage for those unfortunate enough to have been placed on the upper floors.

If I were a foreign tourist bound for Cape Town, I would seriously consider changing my holiday plans – and I imagine that is what many of them will do.

If this were China, someone would have been put up against a wall and shot. If it were Japan, there would have been lots of bowing and an abject apology followed by a ritual disembowelling.

But this is South Africa, and the best we're likely to get is more 'Don't panic' comments from well-paid Eskom execs, idiotic comments from men with sticky-out ears, and a series of expensive adverts (paid for by customers) asking us not to use Eskom's product.

What should happen in a real democracy is that the minister of minerals and energy resigns and the palookas responsible for this debacle are sacked, stripped of their pensions and sent off to the nearest intersection to become squeegee men.

How did it come to this? Well, according to one of the articles I read, it was all because Eskom was expecting 4% economic growth and the hard-working citizens of this country delivered 5%. If they'd known the country's economy was going to grow so fast they would have popped along to Power Stations R Us and snapped up a couple of turbines on special. Have you ever heard such bilge?

A far more likely scenario is this one (but feel free to write in and correct me if you think I'm wide of the mark): When the ANC took over they inherited lots of nasty apartheid legacies, as they never tire of reminding us. They also inherited a few good ones, like a decent road network, dams, some airports and one of the best electricity-supply systems in the world. Admittedly, the supply of electricity in our apartheid years wasn't aimed at the majority of the country's citizens, but you would have thought that the ANC might have realised that and immediately set about increasing capacity to supply their loyal voters some time in the future. Instead, they sacked all the ooms and anyone who reminded them of their oppressive past and replaced them with people who seem very happy to draw salaries of up to R500 000 a month but don't actually know much about electricity. Because the power came whenever you plugged something in, everything was assumed to be fine and money that should have gone towards maintenance and upgrades went, instead, to fat pay-outs for the cronies.

The same criminal neglect applies to the state of our roads, which haven't been properly upgraded since 1994 and are now expected to carry significantly more traffic. However, as there will be no electricity when you get to work it won't matter if you spend five hours in a traffic jam getting there, will it?

Jeeves would show them who's in the driver's seat

19 March 2006

Tucked away on one of the inside pages of *Business Day* last week was a small advertisement calling for the services of a butler/driver.

The successful applicant will speak French and English, hold a valid driver's licence and be able to supply references from previous employers. A fax number is given, along with the warning that should you hear nothing, you can consider your application unsuccessful. Evidently the advertiser is expecting an avalanche of applications.

The requirement for a French speaker rather narrows the possibilities of finding a suitable candidate, I should think. Admittedly, we are a polyglot country, but French is not one of our 11 official languages. So while it would be quite possible for a devious applicant to get hold of a 'valid' driver's licence from those nice Nigerian men in Hillbrow, faking a knowledge of French isn't quite as easy.

Then there's the previous-experience thing. I don't actually know anyone who employs a butler in this country, but that doesn't mean much. Maybe a butler is the latest must-have accessory in the plush suburbs of our great cities, and front doors are now being opened by aloof men in wing collars who insist on announcing visitors. Except we don't have front doors so the butler would have to talk on the intercom to whoever is waiting at the electric front gates, which isn't very butlerish behaviour.

One of the most famous butlers in fiction, PG Wodehouse's Jeeves, certainly wouldn't approve of the advertisement in *Business Day*. More a gentleman's personal gentleman than a run-of-the-mill butler, Jeeves would raise a quizzical eyebrow at the job description butler/driver. His observation would be that you don't ask the chauffeur to pull the cork from the Latour '45 so you shouldn't expect the butler to drive the family limousine, and he would be right.

He would certainly not approve of sending a facsimile, or fax as they are more frequently known.

In the rarefied world of the gentleman's personal gentleman, the usual method of finding a suitable employee is by word of mouth. For example, Old Lord Mough-Dyver dies and his man, Carter, finds himself back in the job market after 45 years of faithful service.

There are always plenty of people eager to snap up the services of a good butler. An interview takes place in which the butler decides whether his potential employee is worthy of his services, rather than the other way round; a blot on the family escutcheon or an unfortunate tendency to be a little bit nouveau riche doesn't go down well.

Once hired, it is the butler's task to let his new master know who is boss. While the employer may like to think he is giving the orders, the truth is that the butler runs the household as he sees fit. The tone of the advertisement in *Business Day* didn't suggest that the new master would appreciate being told what to wear. Jeeves always made it clear to his employer if he didn't approve of certain items of clothing.

Finally, a good butler has to have just the right amount of superciliousness. I would be perfect for this job but I can't speak French.

How to make sure you die owing a lot of dough

26 March 2006

One of the benefits of economic growth is an increase in what the economists like to refer to as 'discretionary income'.

Put simply, this is the chunk of cash left over after you've paid all the necessary monthly expenses. If you're still paying off debt, you don't have genuine discretionary income because anything left over should be put towards reducing your debt. However, if you're in the happy position of having paid off your house and car, and can honestly say that you owe nothing when you receive your pay cheque every month, then you are a legitimate member of the elite discretionary income club.

This enviable state of financial nirvana brings its own problems. If you're saddled with debt then you don't really have any major decisions to make in life. Once you become debt-free you are faced with all sorts of dilemmas. Should you call an investment adviser and put the money to work on the stock exchange? Or should you pop along to The Lounge every week and blow it all on a couple of exotic lap dances? If you invest it successfully, you are faced with an even greater problem because your discretionary income will have grown even larger, and that just makes the problem of what to do with the excess folding stuff even more of a headache.

Everybody should aim to die owing the banks and the government money, and I'm happy to say that the trend of people spending their children's inheritance is growing. Investing discretionary income is a dishonourable cop-out because all it does is give you a bigger final score when 'Game Over' flashes on the monitor screen in the intensive-care unit. What you really need to do with discretionary income is spend it because, by so doing, you will create jobs and wealth and give the rest of us a laugh in the process.

Once you've bought half a dozen wristwatches, a dozen cars, a couple of holiday homes and a wardrobe of tailor-made suits, it probably becomes a bit difficult to know what to buy. Some assets, such as private yachts, are designed to soak up all future discretionary income in running costs, which is why men buy them. They don't enjoy sailing; they simply enjoy owning something that will hoover up cash, thereby freeing them up to look around for a trophy wife.

On a more modest level, those cursed with having to get rid of a chunk of discretionary income every month could do worse than follow the following advice: the first is not to take the word 'discretionary' too seriously.

It implies some degree of responsibility and discrimination, and would, if taken literally, nullify some of life's more entertaining examples of discretionary spending. The second piece of advice is to splash out on something utterly useless. After all, you've got the state-of-the-art cellphone, the latest digital camera, the surround-sound home theatre system and all the iPod paraphernalia, so you have nothing to prove. What you need now is something so unbelievably pointless that it will mark you forever as an extreme discretionary spender. For R1 400 you can buy a full-size, steel copy of Frodo Baggins's sword. I'm told that it even glows blue when Orcs try to hijack your car on Rivonia Road.

Why our paradise is more foolish than real

2 April 2006

It's this column's 12th birthday so I've decided to blow out a few candles. You may have heard the term 'living in a fool's paradise'. It refers to living in a state of delusory happiness and aptly describes the state South Africa finds itself in at the moment.

We kid ourselves that we are experiencing a major economic boom and, thanks to lots of smoke and mirrors, it looks convincing enough. Property prices have risen dramatically, money hasn't been as cheap for more than two decades, tax collection is better than it has ever been and car sales look set for a record third year. So what's there to complain about?

On the surface, nothing, except that little of what we're experiencing makes much sense or is sustainable.

Take property, for example. A two-bedroom townhouse in a fashionable complex that was thrown up in two months costs more than an established house on half an acre 2 km away. If land has an intrinsic value, this doesn't make any sense whatsoever.

Homes in remote but beautiful areas with insufficient water resources sell for millions. Who in their right mind would buy a multimillion-rand property with no regular access to water?

The only reason most people are buying is that they are terrified they will miss out on a great investment opportunity. It's what's known as the greater fool liquidity theory, which dictates that prices level and start falling only when the final sucker in the chain finds he can't sell on at a profit.

The heavy summer rains have exposed the shoddy workmanship of many superficially trendy developments and, surprise, the builders have conveniently gone bust but are busy building elsewhere. While I don't predict a fall in property prices, I do predict a move to quality and value for money, and a R1-million townhouse with paper-thin walls overlooking a busy intersection meets neither of those criteria.

Then there are cars. South Africans still seem to think that a car is an investment, but if you work out the repayment costs and add monthly depreciation, then motoring becomes a very expensive luxury. Just look at the price of one-year-old cars in the newspaper. None of this seems to deter us, though. We continue to buy new cars, even though there are no new roads to drive them on. It makes us feel good.

Meanwhile, our government claims to stand for integrity and swears to weed out corruption, but these are weasel words. According to the auditor-general, 14 Cabinet ministers and deputy ministers and 1 678 provincial ministers and senior public service managers have failed to disclose the pies in which they had their grubby little fingers. If it's true then this is larceny on a grand scale, but hardly surprising in a country in which the deputy president referred to the late Brett Kebble as a great South African and in which the venal members of the ANC Youth League drive around in luxury cars, paid for by the great man.

Beware, the economic boom is nothing more than a chimera designed to deflect attention from the theft and personal enrichment currently taking place in the government and the nationalised industries at your long-term expense.

Fear fuels my civil obedience campaign

9 April 2006

If I'd had most of my assets attached and was facing an expensive and protracted battle in the courts with Pravin Gordhan, I would be worried. The spring in my step would have diminished considerably and my face would have the pallor of a condemned man. Similarly, if I were appearing in court accused of raping an HIV-positive woman or was under investigation by the Scorpions for bypassing the tedious tender process by handing my brother-in-law the contract to upgrade South Africa's mortuaries, a dark cloud would hang over me, my appetite would diminish and I doubt whether I would be getting my full eight hours of uninterrupted sleep.

I am the sort of person who dreads receiving the official envelope telling me that I travelled at 123km/h in a 70km/h zone and must send R1 000 by a date which passed a month ago or risk arrest and anal rape. I don't toss the fine into my glove compartment along with all the others and laugh it off. I make out a cheque immediately and go along to the Post Office and send it registered mail to the municipality. If there were a box on the form asking if I seriously regretted my actions I would undoubtedly tick it.

If my tax assessment takes more than six months I get sweaty palms, even though I know my tax affairs are so straightforward that there can be no possible quibble with what is on the form. In fact, for the past three years, Gordhan's department has sent me money, which means that I have been overpaying tax. I realise that this is not the sort of antisocial behaviour to warrant a mention in dispatches from the deputy president.

I get butterflies in my stomach when confronted with officialdom or the law. After spiders, my greatest fear is litigation and I can think of no greater waste of a life than spending day after day in a musty courtroom. I renew my driver's licence in good time and get panicky if I haven't received a reminder to pay my car's annual licence fee three weeks before it expires. I even overpay the phone bill the month before I go on holiday to avoid getting cut off. I am, in short, a quivering jelly of a man, but at least this civil obedience allows me to lead a moderately stress-free life. Which is why I am so impressed at those who appear to thumb their noses at the law and continue to lead extravagant lifestyles, generally at others' expense.

Last week we reported that Dave King has had many of his assets snatched because he allegedly owes the taxman over R2 billion. Is King holed up in a grubby, rat-infested apartment in Yeoville, weeping about his new state of penury? No, he's in Augusta at the US Masters and evidently regards this latest development as just another blip on life's radar screen.

Isn't it astonishing how so many of those who have been stripped of their assets still manage to live extravagant lifestyles?

Maybe the yawning time gap between accusation and trial encourages them to mock their accusers. Or maybe they just couldn't give a damn because they know they have a better-than-even chance in this country of getting away with their transgressions, particularly if they have powerful and influential friends.

Stupidity a mitigating circumstance for Zuma

16 April 2006

Apart from reinforcing some of those offensive perceptions referred to by President Thabo Mbeki in his speech about black men's sexual appetites and providing endless material for the cartoonists, all the Jacob Zuma rape trial has done is demonstrate how stupid the ex-deputy president really is. I don't mean stupid as in unwise or impetuous or even lacking in the usual quota of brain cells. I mean stupid in the sense of uneducated.

This is hardly Zuma's fault. He grew up without a father and his mother was employed as a domestic worker in Durban, causing him to spend most of his formative years moving between Zululand and the suburbs of Durban.

At the age of 15 he took on odd jobs to supplement his mother's meagre income. As a consequence of this deprived childhood, the young Zuma received no formal schooling. This puts him at a distinct disadvantage compared with many of his political colleagues, particularly those who delight in referring to themselves as intellectuals. Having said that, Zuma was appointed Chief of Intelligence at the ANC-in-exile's head office in Lusaka, so somebody in the organisation clearly thought he was bright enough for the job.

When the ANC came to power in 1994 it was inevitable that a party stalwart and Old Robbenian like Zuma would be rewarded for the 35 years he had loyally devoted to the ANC and Umkhonto weSizwe. His appointment in 1994 as a Member of the Executive Committee of Economic Affairs and Tourism for the KZN provincial government obviously wasn't based on his grasp of economic principles. In fact, it's quite possible that poor Jacob struggled to understand what was going on during the meetings.

But politics is politics and you never turn down the offer of a job just because you haven't a clue what you're doing. If that were the case, there would be an awful lot of unfilled Cabinet positions.

It's easy to snigger at Zuma's comment that he had a shower to minimise the risk of becoming infected with HIV, and to gasp with horror at his implication that women who wear revealing clothing are begging for sex. But, given his lack of formal education and his rural background, we probably wouldn't be surprised to read that he had rubbed his entire body with the fat of a recently slaughtered Nguni bull as protection against sexual disease, bullets, legal action and adverse media comment. And if this were to be the case, is it really any worse than an entire government in denial about AIDS and a Health minister who advocates beetroot and garlic as a remedy? At least Zuma can offer stupidity in mitigation.

A year ago, during the Schabir Shaik trial, Zuma and his supporters were demanding that he have his day in court, which just goes to show that you should be careful what you wish for.

Normally a charge of rape and fraud would be enough to finish a political career, but Zuma's many supporters are proud of their 100% Zuluboy and his rural roots.

Despite his many tribulations, they still regard him as a future president. That's what happens when you hand democracy to people who can barely write their own names.

What we have to suffer now for a job

23 April 2006

Last Sunday an influential London newspaper ran an article calling into question our ability to stage the 2010 Soccer World Cup and suggested that, should we not be up to it, an emergency plan might have to made and the event held in a country of proven competence. Presumably this would rule out England, where they can't even get the iconic Wembley Stadium finished on time.

One of the major quibbles seems to be our complete inability to provide a regular and uninterrupted supply of electricity to the Western Cape. How, they ask, can we be expected to stage an event as important as the World Cup if we don't have enough electricity?

Simple. We'll play all the matches during the day, which will save on floodlights. Always something new out of Africa.

An interesting addendum to that story, and one which is almost certainly going to be snaffled up by a gleeful foreign press, was last week's extraordinary decision by the Cape Arbitration Court which ruled that Eskom was not out of line for employing a black engineer in favour of a better-qualified coloured engineer on the grounds that the former was more previously disadvantaged.

Experts say that the ruling could set a precedent for the Employment Equity Act, and my guess is that it's only a matter of time before new Previously Disadvantaged Assessment Councils (PDACs) are set up at great expense to the taxpayer to assess who has a greater claim to a job they're not really competent to do.

The first hurdle will be the appointment of members of the PDACs and, naturally, preference will be given to those who had to walk 20km to school on dusty roads with bare feet.

Part of the job of a PDAC member will be to examine the past of job applicants before they actually apply for a position. So, for example, anyone applying for the job of removing bolts from generators will first have to get a PDAC clearance certificate which will then be attached to the forged CV and sent to Eskom. No PDAC certificate, no job.

The PDAC clearance certificate will detail the level of disadvantage, and preference will obviously be given to those who experienced a really miserable and deprived childhood.

A points system will apply, and a regular beating and near starvation during childhood will obviously score higher than being made to eat your vegetables and not being allowed to watch *Dallas* on a Tuesday night. Critics of last week's judgment wrongly suggest that this favours blacks over other ethnically and culturally disadvantaged members of society such as Indians, coloureds, the handicapped and white females. If a white female applicant can prove that she had a more disadvantaged past than a black applicant, then there's every chance she will land the job.

Obviously the system is not infallible and there are bound to be those who will claim to have lived in a cardboard box just to land the job of their dreams.

Another idea being mooted is to have another body whose job it would be to decide who shouldn't be entitled to a job based on the fact that their parents bought them a Sony PlayStation2 and an iPod when they were kids.

Spare us the talk of ingratitude, Desmond

30 April 2006

If you happen to have a white skin then you bear two burdens if you live in South Africa. The first is that you are assumed to be racist and therefore unqualified to comment on the widespread corruption, cronyism and incompetence that impedes our development as a nation. The other is that you will always be thought ungrateful for the generosity shown by your black fellow citizens who, out of the goodness of their hearts, didn't drive you into the sea or knock your head off.

This myth of ingratitude was reinforced recently in a speech by Desmond Tutu on the 10th anniversary of the setting up of the shambolic Truth and Reconciliation Commission (TRC), which Tutu chaired. The TRC was supposed to be one of those touchy-feely, nation-healing initiatives set up just after the election in 1994 to help us all come to terms with ourselves. It was unintentionally at the vanguard of reality television and many of you will remember the harrowing scenes of people describing the most terrible events from the apartheid era before tearfully collapsing into the arms of the sympathetic chairman. Oprah would have loved it.

However, what the TRC never managed to do was to bring to book those who had been responsible for such atrocities.

Most whites in South Africa were not directly involved in the apartheid regime, irrespective of whether they voted for the National Party. Like most ordinary citizens they just wanted good schools for their kids, hospitals, roads and a reliable electricity and water supply. In short, they wanted a quiet life and didn't really want to get involved.

When the 1994 elections took place there was surprisingly little right-wing resistance. The whites joined the winding queues and voted and then settled back into the daily routine of going to work, taking the kids to school, filling in their tax forms and all the other mundane minutiae that make up the average suburban lifestyle.

An excited Tutu marvelled that we had managed a peaceful transformation (as did most South Africans) and dubbed us the 'rainbow nation'. So what went wrong and why, 12 years after those elections, are whites still being maligned for not showing enough gratitude? Is it really about gratitude or is it about money?

While the TRC may have provided us with some fine theatre it was pretty ineffectual as a body. Escape deals had obviously been cut with the previous government and promises made not to go for those who had been personally responsible for what happened in the last 10 years of apartheid. Despite the public wailing and gnashing of teeth, the guilty were allowed to retire to their farms or join the funds they had smuggled out of the country. Examples were made of a few of the apartheid henchmen but when it came to extracting the real truth, the TRC was hopelessly inept.

So my message to Desmond Tutu is this: We love you dearly, you are a giant among men, you make us laugh and you make us cry, but if you still believe that whites have not shown enough gratitude towards blacks then perhaps the memory of the sham of the TRC is colouring your judgment.

Visit the Zuma website to see
what was meant

7 May 2006

This week I offer an apology, albeit a qualified one. When I wrote the column on Jacob Zuma 'Stupidity a mitigating circumstance for Zuma' (16 April 2006) I knew it would elicit a response, particularly considering the inflammatory final line. Unfortunately, some of the reaction was from people I hadn't intended to offend but I will return to them later.

The response on the letters page of the *Business Times* reached its nadir last week with one from Clive Swann. Here is a man who glibly speaks of freedom of expression, but only seems to like the concept if the ideas expressed agree with his own. Instead of mounting a rational counter-argument, he resorts instead to gratuitous personal insult and ends up suggesting that Zimbabwe is a safer place to live than England.

Other letters revealed that the writers either hadn't read the article or had completely missed the point, either willfully or unintentionally.

However, the response on the Friends of Jacob Zuma website (www.friendsofjz.co.za) proved the most amusing.

For those of you unfamiliar with this Internet treasure, it is a sort of cyber psychiatric ward for people who still seriously believe that the former deputy president has been set up by the dark forces of government during the recent rape trial; despite him having first denied having sex, being subjected to a DNA test and only then admitting to consensual sex with an HIV-positive house guest half his age.

The messages-of-support page is the one to head for should you be looking for some light amusement. This is a sort of conspiracy theory chat room where delusional inmates can throw themselves against the padded walls without hurting themselves too much.

One of the submissions accuses my grandfather (who never left England) of killing seals in Antarctica and naming a penguin colony after himself.

So, no apologies to the members of Jacob Zuma's Barmy Half-Wits Band (sung to the tune of 'Sgt Pepper's Lonely Hearts Club Band') and none to those readers who couldn't manage a civil letter to this newspaper.

Now to the genuine complainants. A valued friend and colleague expressed unhappiness with the article and was generous enough to explain why there may have been some collateral damage. His first point was the final line – unwittingly lifted from Lady Phillips, as it turns out. That, I was told, would have been construed as racist and being directed at all blacks. Without wishing to equivocate, I don't believe the last line can relate to anything other than the rent-a-rabble Zuma supporters referred to in the previous paragraph.

Another complaint was that the article seemed to demean those with a rural background and chuck them all in the 'stupid' basket. Again, the text of the article (which quotes liberally from the Zuma website) doesn't suggest that to me, but if offence has been taken on either points then I humbly apologise.

As a gesture of atonement I will be sending a cheque for R 5 000 to the one cause that Zuma and his 'burn-the-bitch' mob would find the most repugnant – People Opposing Women Abuse.

At last, I bestow largesse upon poor

14 May 2006

Now that I've become a reconstructed liberal (you see, it was worth writing to the newspaper after all) I've decided that it's time to take on a couple of projects that will assuage my post-colonial white guilt and bring joy and happiness to those less fortunate in the hopes that, together, we can build a stronger nation.

Such philanthropy doesn't come cheap, and I've been casting around for a dodgy millionaire or two to help me out with some cash-flow problems. Sadly, all the available dodgy millionaires seem to have been snaffled by senior politicians so the newly launched Out to Lunch Foundation (OtLF) may have to lower its sights somewhat.

Like Bono and Bob Geldof, I had hoped to get off to a good start by persuading finance houses to waive the monthly repayments on all cars costing less than R400 000.

Unfortunately, with no fat-wallet backers, the Foundation has had to abandon this demand for debt relief. For much the same reason I've also had to jettison plans to rally South African musicians, hire a studio and record 'Do They Know it's Mother's Day?' as a fundraising bestseller. It's a crying shame, because we had hoped to devote the entire sales proceeds to communities that have to survive on a diet of potato crisps and fizzy American drinks bought from the corner café. The Foundation would have sent carers into the affected areas to explain that fizzy drinks can rot your teeth, leaving you with a gummy smile at age 24, and that monosodium glutamate from the crisps can seriously impair your judgment as to who might make a suitable president when Thabo Mbeki goes off to run the UN in a couple of years.

So, compared with the Bill and Melinda Gates Foundation, the OtLF gets off to a precarious start, but I'm determined not to allow a lack of funding to scupper my dreams. Bill and Melinda have devoted themselves to the eradication of malaria; Bono and Bob are attempting to get the rich nations to give the poor nations a break before they force more money on them; and all beauty queens are striving for world peace. So what can the OtLF do that will be meaningful and inexpensive?

I poured myself a large Glenmorangie Madeira Wood Finish, lit a Hoyo Epicure 1 and pondered the problem. It came to me in a flash. As the Arbitration Court recently ruled, the most deserving people in this country are the previously disadvantaged.

So the challenge was simple. What could the OtLF provide to make the previously disadvantaged feel better about themselves?

The answer is Su Doku puzzles with only one number to fill in. Or crosswords with simple three-letter clues. You know how frustrating Su Doku can be sometimes? Well, you need never get frustrated again, thanks to the OtLF.

It's not about race, but about attitude

21 May 2006

Arecurring accusation in the hate mail I have been receiving over the past few weeks is that I am arrogant and think I am better than other people. Therein lies the clue to many of the problems in this country.

I admit I leap out of bed every morning in the belief that South Africa is lucky to have me as a taxpayer and that my contributions to various publications greatly enrich the lives of thousands of people. That you may violently disagree with this is of no consequence. The point is I believe it and that's what motivates me to sit in front of a blank computer screen every week trying to think of something original to write. So I'm afraid your repeated attempts to knock me off my pedestal are in vain.

Contrast this abundant self-confidence with the born-loser complex of many of my detractors and you begin to realise that this country's problems are not racial but attitudinal. If you are encouraged by politicians to spend your life blaming the past for your lack of opportunity, the chances are that you will achieve little. You must also understand that, in the event of non-delivery, it's in the politician's best interest to blame the previous regime for everything.

The history of mankind is one of subjugation and that's not about to change. One group dominates another either for economic or religious reasons, or simply to show who's boss. My lot were invaded by some uninvited Romans in 55BC but we'd also had the Vikings to contend with and, much later, the Normans. The victim mentality hadn't been discovered then, so the Saxons just had to get on with life and adapt to the ways of their conquerors.

Times and terminology have changed and subjugation is now carried out under the euphemisms of 'liberation' and 'peace keeping', but its ultimate aim is the same: to make sure the masses do what they're told.

In 1994 we were told that a miracle had happened in South Africa. We held elections for a truly democratic government. People were free at last to better themselves. Some have done so and look what has happened to them. They are labelled sell-outs and coconuts by the envious, baying mob. It's apparently quite acceptable for no-hopers to take large amounts of money from crooked businessman, but if you study hard and go on to make a fortune then you risk alienation. Thankfully, this cultural tall-poppy syndrome hasn't deterred those determined to see 1994 as an opportunity for real change and not just a date in our country's history.

An added insult is the assumption that black people succeed only because of the colour of their skin and their previous level of disadvantage. This is pernicious nonsense, but few are likely to believe otherwise while the government and industrial courts agree to build a new society based on the lowest common denominator.

Write to complain if you must, but I know I'm right.

The natives on the President's shoulder

28 May 2006

So they do have a sense of humour, after all. No, I'm not referring to the fact that media celebs Vuyo Mbuli and Tim Modise have been invited to become members while people like writer John Matshikiza and *Sunday Times* editor Mondli Makhanya are still waiting patiently for their application forms to arrive.

I'm referring to the Native Club, the name chosen for the group of black intellectuals who will, er ... well now, I'm not quite sure what their role will be. I may have read it somewhere but it obviously didn't strike me as important enough to file away.

Ah yes, it's coming back to me. They will, in the words of chief native (it feels so naughty to write that) Titus Mofolo, 'seek to build a climate congenial to continued reflection and self-examination by the native intelligentsia, asserting itself in the realms of arts and culture, socio-economy and politics'.

What the hell does that mean? Well, you know what intellectuals are like. If they can say something plainly in 10 words then you can be sure they will put it in at least 30 words that nobody can understand.

It's been suggested that Mofolo's close proximity to the corridors of power (he's political adviser to the President) could indicate that the Native Club will perform an influential advisory role to the government, filling the many intellectual voids that exist.

This probably explains the absence of what are scornfully termed neo-liberal blacks, whose principal aim in life is to shape the transformation of South Africa for their own selfish ends.

Fortunately, the Native Club will be made up of trustworthy black intellectuals and definitely not the sort of riff-raff who call into question government policy or, heaven forbid, suggest publicly that the ANC is currently experiencing leadership difficulties.

While it's tremendously comforting to learn that only those driven by the purest of motives will qualify for membership of this elite club, there are critics (probably the aforementioned neo-libs) who scoff that the Native Club is nothing but a latter-day Broederbond made up of brown-nosed sycophants.

The ANC government is well known for reacting poorly to criticism. Indeed, so arrogant and power-hungry has it become that it's not prepared to vacate Cape Town's municipal offices, even though it was defeated fairly in an election.

So a group of fawning intellectuals would be great to have around in times of strife. It reminds me of those old Disney films where there was always some smarmy creature sitting on a shoulder of the villain, whispering encouragement.

The problem comes when the yes men have too much sway and suggest clamping down on things like freedom of speech and the media.

Maybe it would be a good idea to start the Soutie Club, the Coon Club, the Coolie Club and the Rock-Spider Club as a sort of intellectual antidote to the Natives. You never know when they might get restless.

It was fun in the sun while it lasted

4 June 2006

I was thumbing through my dog-eared copy of Edmund Burke's *Reflections on the Revolution in France* when a thought struck me: Why hasn't the ANC managed to create a larger black middle class in the 12 years it has been in power? Surely that was what Codesa was all about in the run-up to the election? Wasn't the deal that the whiteys hand over power without a fight in return for hanging on to most of their money and not having their throats slit? Well, something along those lines.

Wealth could then be redistributed in an orderly fashion and the economy would boom for everyone as compensation. The pain the whites would feel by sharing the nation's wealth for the first time in their lives would be eased by a bull market. Well, we've had the bull market, property has boomed and we all like to think we're much richer than we were 12 years ago, but what we have failed to take into account is this one-man, one-vote thing, which could blow all our dreams away.

If, instead of creating a small mega-rich elite, the ANC had stuck to the original plan and seen to it that more of its constituents became substantially better off, we would probably not be facing the problems we face today.

As things stand, though, there is a large, resentful underclass that feels it has been short-changed these past 12 years while others have evidently grown immensely wealthy at its expense.

Since we all have the same voting rights, it seems obvious that the majority of poor, semi-literate and unemployed voters will wield far more power at the next election than the minority of wealthy, literate and employed voters. Unlike shares, your democratic votes are not linked to how much money you have invested in SA Inc.

The less-educated voter is easily swayed by the promise of better times ahead. A man who has no job and no decent home to call his own really hasn't too much to lose; if his first party of choice has failed to deliver on its pre-election promises, then he will almost certainly vote for somebody else. If their promises turn out to be as empty as the previous government's, then he is no worse off.

This reality should send a shiver down the spines of those who believe South Africa has turned into a sun-baked version of the smarter parts of Europe.

Our property market may be buoyant, but many of those magnificent houses you see in the glossy property pages are not being built for people who live in tin shacks. They're being built as second or third homes for people who already have a magnificent first home. They stand tantalisingly empty for most of the year, their very existence mocking the poor and the homeless.

A populist leader swept to power by the angry mob would become even more popular by handing out uninhabited homes to his loyal supporters.

It couldn't happen here, though, could it? You bet it could. Who's going to stop it? An underpaid and demotivated police force? A security guard earning R1 000 a month? We're about to fulfil the old Chinese curse of living in interesting times. Still, the party was fun while it lasted.

Money tree grows at Rosebank intersection

11 June 2006

I got done for not stopping at a stop sign the other day. Obviously I argued the case with the Metro Police officer while another 28 drivers (I counted) who also hadn't stopped drove past unhindered by other Metro officers doing a fair impression of Lord Nelson at Trafalgar.

'How long am I expected to stop for?' I asked. There was no adequate answer to the question so I explained that I have fast reactions and had stopped long enough to notice there was no traffic coming from the right or from ahead.

She wasn't buying that so I suggested she just write the ticket for R500, which is the fine for not stopping at a stop sign. If you travel without number plates, thereby making your car unidentifiable in a hit-and-run or to a speed camera, the fine is only R400.

So if I'd had no number plates I could have just driven past the Metro officer, turned down a side street and saved myself R500. A fine example of the law being a complete ass.

Apart from the stopping time being at the discretion of the Metro officer, I have another objection. This particular stop street is at a junction near the *Sunday Times* offices in Rosebank.

It is a relic of history because the road that fed in from the right has been closed for years to allow for the building of the Rosebank Mall pedestrian precinct.

So the only traffic coming from the right at that stop sign is the odd car leaving the underground parking at the local FNB branch, in which case you can see the boom is up and you obviously stop.

The road ahead is also closed off and is a parking lot for about 10 cars at most. The area is secured by removable metal posts so, again, it's easy to see if there's traffic coming your way. There is a pedestrian crossing at the stop sign and obviously you are going to stop if someone is crossing the road.

However, there's absolutely no reason to stop and sit in your car for even 30 seconds at this intersection just to impress a Metro cop, because there isn't usually any traffic.

Which makes it the ideal place to trap, because what is common sense to a driver is not necessarily common sense to a cop armed with a fine book.

There were six Metro officers on duty that day. The officer who stopped me told me she usually gets through a whole book of 200 fines a day.

Let's assume her colleagues are as successful. That's R600 000 a day, or R12 million a month, they collect – if they are there only on weekdays. Even if they have a slack month, they probably still rake in R4 million, which must make the corner of Tyrwhitt and Cradock avenues some of the most profitable undeveloped real estate around.

About 200 m away is a taxi rank. I walked through it later that day and counted at least four major transgressions, including almost bald tyres. Not surprisingly, there wasn't a cop in sight.

While I'm delighted to see the Metro Police establishing a greater presence on our streets, I can't help thinking that a more broad-based system of policing might be preferable.

But would it be as profitable for the municipality?

Cracked old chinas fill up the Cabinet

18 June 2006

Chris Barron's recent *Sunday Times* obituary of Stella Sigcau, minister of Public Works, is a sorry reminder that, even 12 years after the advent of democracy in this country, many Cabinet portfolios are handed out as a reward for struggle loyalty and not because the President believes the person can do the job effectively.

To quote Barron's delicious prose on Sigcau: 'Her veins ran with East Pondoland royal blood, but that was about the only movement one could readily associate with her statuesque person; as a minister in three post-apartheid governments she seemed to be so inactive that it was easy to forget her existence. When she was remembered it was only to ask why she was still in the government.

'The only plausible answer was that the ANC needed her to keep traditional leaders onside and deliver the votes of communities in the once quite hotly contested rural areas of the Eastern Cape.'

Her entire period of high office was characterised by inactivity ('If you give a job to Stella Sigcau, nothing happens,' sighed insiders, many of them in her own department), accusations of bribery, suggestions of unauthorised spending, failure to follow correct tender procedures and general financial chicanery. Needless to say, the accusations didn't bother her or affect her career because, like so many of our politicians, she evidently regarded accountability as a quaintly Eurocentric concept and quite unsuitable for a thriving African democracy.

I met Sigcau once. I had been invited onto Felicia Mabuza-Suttle's talk show as the token white man to tell the audience that affirmative action was nothing more than an insulting form of tokenism.

Actually, I wasn't the only whitey. My fellow panellist was from a rival Sunday newspaper but when I noticed he was wearing suede shoes I knew I would be on my own. Naturally, Sigcau and I disagreed, so after the show I went up to shake her hand to show there were no hard feelings just because I was right and she was wrong. She refused to shake hands and instead made grunting noises, which I put down to surliness.

Rewarding political allies is commonplace and was to be expected when the ANC came to power. But surely we are entitled to expect better management 12 years down the line? Particularly as some government departments are so well run and have been for many years.

The Finance portfolio immediately springs to mind and one wonders what people like Trevor Manuel think when they are forced to sit around a Cabinet table with those who are, to put it mildly, hideously out of their depth. I guess we won't know until his memoirs are published.

Minister of Safety and Security Charles Nqakula's recent comments on crime make him sound a bit like Basil Fawlty, but they are really a cry for help. What the whinger speech did was to send a signal which said 'Help, I haven't a clue what I'm doing and I want an easier job'. Instead of mocking the poor man and encouraging other whingers to write to the letters page, the media should be scouting around for a competent replacement for poor confused Nqakula.

Throw hijackers and rapists to the lions

25 June 2006

Reading our newspapers you can't help wondering whether South Africans have a natural talent for crime, particularly violent crime. Some countries are known for their cooking and some for their football skills but South Africa's reputation overseas usually has something to do with murder and mayhem. The muesli munchers (Lefties) will probably say it's all because of poverty, but that's far too simplistic an explanation.

Survival crimes, like cellphone theft, muggings and burglaries, happen all over the world, although they are not committed only for survival reasons; some people simply get a buzz out of petty crime.

However, I have yet to discover a country that has quite the appetite South Africa has for child and baby rape and for sickening and brutal murder. Again, the muesli munchers will blame apartheid, crowded townships, low employment and whatever else they can dream up. The real explanation, of course, is much simpler; this country is soft on crime.

When striking security guards first trashed the Johannesburg CBD, and were caught doing so on camera, the authorities announced that no action would be taken against them. I'm sure this was intended as a gesture of goodwill, offered in the hope of easing a tense standoff between employers and employees, but it backfired badly. It was seen by the strikers as carte blanche to be as lawless as they wished without fear of prosecution.

When a government gives up law enforcement or is simply too wet to introduce measures urgently needed to curb serious crime, then law-abiding citizens should be worried.

Crime, like legitimate business, is all about risk and reward. If the risk of being caught or successfully prosecuted is low and the rewards are high, then obviously it makes sense to become a criminal. If raping a three-week-old baby is your thing and you know the punishment doesn't fit the crime then why not go ahead and satisfy your desires? And if putting a bullet in the head of a young mother as the grand finale to a car hijacking makes your day, then go right ahead because you'll just become a police docket number.

It's no coincidence that crime is lowest in countries that punish criminals with great severity. Singapore can be criticised as somewhat anodyne but at least you can walk the streets at night. For Singaporeans crime simply doesn't pay. The same applies in Dubai.

South Africa urgently needs to bring back the death penalty for a range of serious crimes, but it's unlikely to happen because the anti-death penalty activists argue that a man doesn't have the right to take the life of another man, no matter how evil he has been.

So how about this for a solution? Drop convicted criminals in the Kruger Park 20 km from the nearest camp on a night with no moon. If they survive until morning then they go free.

If they end up as a lion's main course or get trampled by elephants then put it down to the will of a greater power. A uniquely South African answer to a uniquely South African problem.

And think how much more exciting night drives would be.

Face the facts: it's time to switch, Blade

2 July 2006

Blade Nzimande, the general secretary of the SA Communist Party, is obviously not as sharp as his name suggests. Writing on the SACP's website under the portentous title 'Red Alert', he takes to task various columnists, myself included, warning of the 'creeping danger among sections of our intellectuals, through some of their pronouncements and paradigmatic assumptions, of creating a climate of anti-intellectualism'.

While I'm quite happy for Cde Nzimande to take issue with whatever I write, I have to object in the strongest possible terms at being labelled an 'intellectual', even if only by implication.

Whether Cde Nzimande is being gratuitously cruel or simply bandying the word around without thinking too much is not important. What is important is that he withdraw this slander immediately. If my readers start perceiving me as an intellectual my days as a lifestyle columnist are numbered.

Although I've never met the man, I have a feeling that Cde Blade and I would hit it off rather well over lunch at the Rand Club. He is, after all, passionate about the lost cause of communism and I always enjoy the company of people of passion.

I had to study *The Communist Manifesto* for A level and was greatly impressed by the ideology of communism until I spent a few minutes thinking about it and realised that man is far too interesting a creature to want to be like all other men.

We are ambitious: we want to be faster, better, richer, sexier and cleverer than the common herd, which is why communism can never really work. Its appeal lies with life's losers, who take great comfort from the belief that they are being exploited by the wicked owners of the means of production. It never seems to dawn on them that without these wicked business owners they wouldn't even have jobs and would starve to death.

Putting the means of production in the hands of the people's government doesn't really work either. Communists by their very nature are not the sort of people to go the extra mile so anything run by communists is usually a collective disaster.

The shelves in the stores are empty, nothing works properly, everyone has to drive a car made out of cardboard and the women age prematurely, grow beards and lose their teeth by the time they're 40. While all this is happening the party officials raid the coffers to give themselves a substantially better lifestyle than the misery they have visited on their citizens. Is this really the sort of society Cde Nzimande wants?

Apart from being in a good position to pick up a lot of cut-price hammer-and-sickle T-shirts and other redundant commie paraphernalia, one can't really see the point of the continued existence of the SACP, other than as a comic sideshow and a haven for malcontents.

The Berlin Wall came down in 1989, Russia dumped communism as unworkable more than a decade ago and China looks pretty capitalist to me.

Let the trend be your friend, Blade. Come and have lunch and let me persuade you to switch allegiance.

SABC news has never been better

9 July 2006

I stopped watching SABC news long ago. My decision had nothing to do with perceptions of pro-ruling party bias on my part. It was quite simply a matter of timing. Rival station e.tv opted to broadcast its evening news bulletin at 7pm and so SABC3 decided to move its bulletin from 8pm to 7pm to compete directly for viewers.

Since I'm usually doing something much more important at 7pm, I hardly ever watch the SABC news. Which means that I'm not at all well qualified to enter the great SABC news debate except to point out the obvious and wonder whether we aren't all making a fuss about nothing.

The SABC has always been the government's official mouthpiece and there are some among us who clearly remember a man called PW Botha phoning the honchos of the SABC in the afternoon to demand airtime that very night. Instead of the expected episode of *Dallas*, we would be treated to the sight of a man with a very slobbery lower lip and a wagging finger rambling on about how certain people in his own party were out to get him.

In fairness to the new order, I have no recollection of any current Cabinet minister demanding airtime in this way. In fact, many would argue that our President could benefit from rather more television exposure than he enjoys. Since there seems to be little, if any, evidence of direct political manipulation when it comes to what goes out under the guise of SABC news one must assume that the problem lies within the SABC.

Is it not possible that, in their eagerness to please their political masters, some of those employed to bring us the news on state TV are simply a bunch of treacly-mouthed sycophants who would be extremely unlikely to find employment as journalists elsewhere? That doesn't necessarily make them bad people, but it does throw a huge question mark over their journalistic integrity.

But since when has being an embedded journalist been a crime?

The government advertised a couple of years ago for membership of its press corps and I doubt a qualification would have been a 12-year track record as a politically incorrect columnist for the best-selling newspaper in the country. So I saved them the embarrassment of having to pretend I wasn't quite what they were looking for by not even applying.

If the SABC were to suddenly start broadcasting documentaries about President Thabo Mbeki we would either assume that a third force bent on ousting the great Web trawler had taken over at the SABC or that the doccie had been sanitised by the SABC censors. So, in a way, the poor old state broadcaster is damned either way.

I'm genuinely surprised that anyone believes they should hear or see the unvarnished truth from the SABC, which is precisely why certain official spokesmen are favoured and others banned. You only have to look at the membership of the SABC board news committee to realise that the official version of the news needs to be taken with a large-ish measure of salt.

But that's why you have an off button on your TV remote.

Why Zuma makes me sit bolt upright

16 July 2006

I don't know how good you feel about a man with presidential ambitions singing 'Bring me my machine gun' at political rallies. I don't mind admitting that it scares the hell out me.

Machine guns are a very effective way of settling scores and Mr Jacob Zuma certainly gives the impression of being a man with a lot of scores to settle if and when he becomes president.

We already have some idea of what press freedom would be like under Zuma; namely, non-existent. Like Mad Bob up north, poor old vain JZ wants media that will flatter him.

He may be attempting to sue us for damage to his reputation now, but I suspect from the gleam in his eye that a preferable solution would be 3 000 volts through the genitals or the Argentine alternative whereby journalists just don't turn up for work one day and are never seen again.

There's no shortage of nutters in the JZ camp, as was demonstrated recently on a phone-in radio programme. Some of them can barely muster enough brain power to keep their vital organs functioning.

I'm sure they'd be more than happy to form death squads to rid this fair land of all those who have belittled their hero and attempted to prevent his rise to greatness.

As you probably know, Zuma has redefined optimism and is suing various members of the media for amounts of money they would be unlikely to earn in several lifetimes. He wants R6 million from me, but his lawyers haven't specified exactly what it was in two of my columns that upset him so I haven't felt justified in writing the cheque.

Since neither contained anything remotely defamatory, my guess is that he objected to being called stupid. As this is common cause anyway I can't see what all the fuss is about.

It's well known that ambitious, stupid men generally keep the company of those either as stupid or even more stupid than themselves because that's the way they look good. But it's not just the gormless that JZ gathers around him. If you look at his support base you cannot fail to notice that it includes convicted fraudsters, discredited ex-journalists, dubious legal and financial advisers, recipients of largesse from the late Brett Kebble and sundry half-wit rent-a-gobs who will back Zuma solely for what he might give them should he ever (heaven forbid) come to power. Unfortunately, history shows that even stupid men can be swept to power on a wave of populism, particularly when the rest of society are busy congratulating themselves on how rich they have become or tell themselves that it couldn't happen here.

While I totally support Zuma's right to use the courts if he genuinely believes he has been wronged, I don't think he has a bat's hope in hell of funding his political ambitions at the expense of people like me. I also can't imagine that the spectre of press censorship will do much to enhance South Africa's reputation in the world.

Jacob Zuma would do the whole country a favour by opting for retirement. Will he do it? Probably not. Encouraged by his ability to get an erection at age 63, he now probably believes anything is possible – including that he can still become president.

Here's looking at you, South Africa

23 July 2006

President Mbeki has already warned naysayers that any negativity over our ability to stage a gobsmackingly brilliant World Cup in 2010 will be punished under the Saying Rotten things About South Africa Act 2006 (as amended).

So I was mortified to read in the white-owned press (including my own organ) adverse comments about our 49-0 drubbing in Brisbane last weekend. I really think we need to try harder to put a positive slant on this.

What I know about rugby is roughly equivalent to what John Robbie knows about opera. But that doesn't mean that I cannot weep patriotic crocodile tears. Come on guys ... we could have been beaten 52-0 or even 90-0 but we weren't and that's because our team have been specially selected for damage limitation. Convinced? Neither am I, so it's back to the presidential edict not to say anything nasty about our capacity to stage the world's greatest sports event bar none in 2010.

The R Slickers have been writing to the press saying that we staged the 1995 Rugby World Cup and the 2001 Global Underwater Orienteering Championships and nobody said we couldn't do it then.

Which means that those who say we will struggle to find enough rickshaws to get fans to the matches in 2010 are deliberately dissing us because they are racist.

Well, maybe they are – but if the ANC still haven't learnt to take criticism from the people who pay their salaries after 12 years then we are in serious trouble.

For the record, I think the 2010 World Cup is a good thing for South Africa, even if half the foreign fans get hijacked or murdered, have to cycle to the matches and watch play by the light of miners' lamps because Eskom has run out of power.

It doesn't matter if we cock it up because for the next few years and many years after we will be the focus of a sports-mad world.

Now, the Middle East may be trying to steal our thunder by bombing the hell out of each other, but experience tells us this phase will soon pass and be replaced by single-digit daily deaths and casualties.

We will feature once again in the world's crystal ball. They will ask again and again whether we are up to the task of staging the 2010 Cup. They will question who the president could be in 2010. They will question our ability to curb violent crime and will wonder aloud whether to issue a travel advisory to any of their citizens planning to visit South Africa without a personal bodyguard or their own standing army.

The answers to the above are irrelevant because what really matters is that, for the next four years, we will be talked about. We will be scrutinised by a cynical world and that has to be good for all South Africans.

Maybe our politicians will choose their company more carefully, hanging out with respected business figures rather than philanthropic gangsters.

Perhaps the minister of transport will awake from his long slumber and introduce new laws to test the roadworthiness of cars.

We all know we haven't a hope of winning the 2010 World Cup, but if hosting it keeps some of our politicians on the straight and narrow for a few years, it will have been worth the effort.

Painting the façade as building burns

30 July 2006

My hypothetical toilet cistern is cracked, the roof in the main bed-room leaks when it rains and the kitchen cupboard doors have fallen off their hinges.

Not ideal conditions for hassle-free living, I'm sure you would agree. Suddenly I win R20 000 on the lottery; more than enough to sort out my immediate domestic problems.

So what do I do? I rush out and buy a large plasma television screen that I hope will impress my friends. After all, they're not going to see the leaking roof in the bedroom or the cracked toilet cistern, and I'll just tell them I'm in the process of changing the kitchen cupboard doors if they're rude enough to ask. This is pretty much what is happening with the renaming of our main international airport.

Now before all you splenetic new democracy patriots write in to tell me that OR Tambo was the greatest struggle personality of all time, al-low me to put your minds at rest by telling you that I don't give a fig what you call the airport.

As it is, I can neither remember, spell nor pronounce most of the new names you've already come up with, so in my household we will contin-ue to refer to it as 'the airport'. Fortunately, I have a satellite navigation system in my car that isn't bamboozled by all these new appellations, so when I see the turn-off for something called OR Tambo I won't think I've got the wrong airport.

The obvious name for our main airport would have been Nelson Mandela International and I doubt we would have heard a peep from the paler element of the population if this had been the case. But the personable Dr Pallo Jordan, our Arts and Culture minister, has pointed out that Nelson Mandela is already a square, an informal settlement, a municipality, a bay and a block of flats in London, England, which is why he can't also be an international airport. I mean, fair's fair and all that.

I expect there's a rule within the ANC saying that you can't be named after more than four separate amenities.

So our international airport will become OR Tambo International and the vast cost of changing the name on everything from road signs to stationery will get under way.

As a political activity, name-changing is a darned sight easier than creating job opportunities, sorting out crime, making sure the roads are safe and providing healthcare.

This is obviously why so many ANC members attack the job with such gusto and waste an enormous amount of time trying to think of names that will particularly annoy the honkies.

Apart from the fact that a whole bunch of fat-cat politicians are being paid to do nothing but think up new names for things, there is the cost factor to consider. If everyone in the country had a home, food and running water and we were crime-free, then squandering public funds on what is little more than a massive ego trip might be justifiable.

But they don't and so it isn't.

It's just another slap in the face for the poor who are, admittedly, pretty used to being slapped in the face by the ruling party. Maybe living in a place with an inoffensive name reduces the pangs of hunger.

Political correctness just brown-nosing

6 August 2006

I have never had much time for political correctness and have frequently gone out of my way in this column to be politically incorrect just for the hell of it.

The sort of people who support political correctness usually have little sense of how ridiculous the whole PC thing is, which is why they are precisely the sort of people one should mock mercilessly in a newspaper column.

For example, who in their right mind would use the term 'differently abled' to describe a person crippled in a road accident?

Not that the inventors of politically correct words aren't without imagination and even an involuntary sense of irony. I'm sure anyone living in a former squatter camp would be chuffed to learn that they are now living in an informal settlement. Just as all those persons of colour who try to sell us plastic coat hangers, alternatively produced DVDs and tubes of superglue at busy intersections must thank their lucky stars that they are not melanin deprived because, if they were, they would be charged with jaywalking.

While some of the more absurd politically correct euphemisms may be good for a laugh, the real danger lies not in your use of the right words but in your attitude.

It's become an Orwellian thought crime. Political correctness is really just an insidious form of censorship, but it's cunning censorship because it implies you are a poor citizen if you still use certain words and phrases, and have the wrong sort of thoughts in your head.

The creeping tentacles of political correctness have been attempting to strangle freedom of expression for the past 12 years. A mainly black government suddenly taking over from a totally white government was an obvious recipe for the race-card defence of incompetence.

Thus, when anyone with a pale skin criticises a government official it is put down to racism and nothing more need be said. I've often tried to explain to people that stupidity, dishonesty and incompetence are not gender or race specific and that there are plenty of white-skinned contenders. Indeed, one of our biggest post-democracy fraudsters was white.

So how can pointing out the incompetence of politicians be construed as racist simply because they have black skin?

To be accused of racism, of not embracing the new South Africa, is, in many people's minds, the equivalent of being accused of being a child molester.

But it's not only the stigma of being thought politically incorrect that makes otherwise intelligent people behave like zombies. The stick of the stigma is augmented by the carrot of financial reward, particularly if you happen to be a large company looking for government contracts. The contortions some companies attempt to please our political masters would have done Harry Houdini proud.

What we really need in South Africa are business leaders who are bold enough to tell the politicians the harsh truth occasionally instead of constantly doffing their caps and doing whatever they are told; people who can stand up to a politician's bullying.

What we have at the moment is a nation of grovelling corporate yes men terrified to voice their real opinions in public for fear their massive bonuses may be affected.

Talk to them in private, though, and you hear a different story.

Even Mbeki can't tame the Sultans of Bling

13 August 2006

It's all very well President Mbeki eloquently lamenting our culture of greed in his recent Nelson Mandela lecture; but isn't he about 10 years too late?

Where was the calm voice of reason when the snouts were pushing roughly towards the BEE swill trough? Was there any restraint shown then or any censure for comments such as 'Blacks should get filthy rich' and 'I didn't join the struggle to be poor'? Well if there was, I didn't notice it.

When the embarrassingly gormless leaders of the ANC Youth League received such largesse from that infamous nocturnal aviator, Brett Kebble, did they: a) give it to the poor; b) rush out to buy sharp suits and fast cars; or c) start a foundation providing primary healthcare to rural communities?

Obviously the answer is b, and for a very good reason. If you're an aspirational Sultan of Bling and somebody gives you a pile of free money, it would be pointless to waste it on the poor. After all, as the Bible teaches, the poor are always with us and there's nothing a poor man likes more than to see a fellow member of the previously disadvantaged strutting around in a tailor-made suit and edging the donkey carts off the road in his overpowered car. It gives people hope. Apparently.

Then there's this ubuntu thing, which is a bit confusing if you're white. It may sound like the name of an aftershave but it actually refers to humanity towards others. White capitalism allows you to tread the faces of the poor into the dirt in your quest for greater riches, but black capitalism has this ubuntu thing, which is a bit like a speed regulator on a BMW that stops you from travelling faster than 250km/h.

The idea is that the ubuntu regulator kicks in and says something like, 'Hey there, big boy. You've already made R700 million this year, don't you think you should leave something for someone else?'

However, rather like the speed regulator on the BMW, ubuntu can also be overridden if you know how.

What puzzles me about the accumulation of great wealth is why we all get so worked up about it. Money begets money and if you're even relatively well-off and debt-free your investments should generate more cash than you can ever hope to spend. So the rich are bound to get richer through no fault of their own.

Believe it or not, wealth becomes a burden. Once you have all life's necessities such as a surround-sound home theatre, a wine cellar for 6 000 bottles and a helipad, you run out of things to spend money on.

Take poor old Dave King. Reports suggest the beleaguered billionaire spent R1 million a month. How do you spend that kind of money unless you use seven-ply toilet paper, eat foie gras for every meal and fly Eric Clapton in every week to give you guitar lessons?

In the end, though, it all comes down to sex. We buy things we don't need because they are part of our breeding plumage. A flashy car and a diamond-encrusted watch send a signal to the opposite sex that says: 'Please mate with me because I can compensate you financially for my lack of personality.'

Now the ball's well and truly rolling, the desire for wealth at the expense of spiritual development is unlikely to diminish because of a presidential slap on the wrist.

Brace yourself as air travel hits new lows

20 August 2006

Air travel will never be the same again. No, I'm not talking about the possibility of being blown up in midair by suicide bombers who've smuggled something on board. That would all be over in seconds and would be annoying only in the sense that you'd never get to see the end of the in-flight movie.

I'm talking about something far more horrific and torturous, and that is the prospect of having to travel on long-haul flights with none of the things that make air travel slightly more bearable, such as iPods, deodorant, toothpaste, a spare shirt and a laptop computer.

The poor sods who turned up at Heathrow on the day of the scare, to be told they were allowed to board with only the bare essentials in a see-through plastic bag and would have to squeeze everything else of value into their main luggage or throw it away, showed typical British resolve.

In other words, they were prepared to believe whatever they were told by a government well known for its duplicity.

What I find interesting is that it was only the unholy alliance of Bush and Blair that recognised this new threat from Muslim fundamentalists. For the most part other European airports carried on with business as usual.

I'm not normally one for conspiracy theories, but when it comes to Bush and Blair I concede that it's quite possible they concocted the whole airliners-being-blown-up-in-midair story to detract from their botched attempts at trying to bring peace to the Middle East, while at the same time ensuring a plentiful supply of oil at the right price.

On the other hand, British intelligence may have just saved the world. You choose.

The problem now is whether we will survive on an airline-entertainment diet of tired old comedy radio shows and outdated movies shown on flickering screens. And have you ever tried to get a cup of water from the cabin staff at three in the morning? That's why smart people bring their own.

What will become of the duty-free shops if we're not allowed to take our treasured bottle of Glenmorangie Madeira Wood Finish on board, and will there be a thriving secondary market in stolen laptops and iPods?

I've already heard one story of an executive – on his way to South Africa to present the board with sensitive information – arriving without his laptop, which had mysteriously gone missing.

It's all too ghastly to contemplate and, given the choice of being blown up in midair versus having to survive a 10-hour flight without my personal survival kit, I'd opt for being blown up any day – just so long as I didn't know about it before boarding.

It took nearly two years for metal knives to make a comeback after 9/11, and some airlines still use plastic. So I doubt whether personal items of cabin comfort such as moisturising creams, drinking water and eye drops will be allowed back too soon.

Which means that you now pay a fortune to an airline to be treated like a criminal on arrival at the airport and transported like a refugee. If I wanted that sort of humiliation I'd prefer to take my chances with Fiona Coyne on *The Weakest Link*.

President's golf pals are pro schmoozers

27 August 2006

I didn't crack an invitation to the Friends of the President Golf Day last week at the Pretoria Country Club. I like to think this is because my legendary golfing skills still go unrecognised in the corridors of power.

I once scored a hole-in-one on the seventh at the Brighton Crazy Golf Course which, while it may not be St Andrews, has one of the trickiest miniature hump-backed bridges I have encountered. Not only did I score a hole-in-one but I did it while holding a stick of candyfloss in my left hand; something not even Tiger Woods can do.

The only other possibility is that I'm not yet considered a friend of the President, despite the sage advice I have been giving him for free since he came to power.

It's a funny name for a golf day, isn't it? They could have just called it the President's Golf Day and no one would have bothered to comment. Apart, that is, from all the loony Lefties and commies in Cosatu who regard golf as the game of their oppressors. I've often thought that it must be a miserable existence to be a Leftie because practically everything smacks of oppression and unfairness to them.

It's an enormous burden to carry through life because every morning you are obliged to get out of bed and think of something else to be enraged about.

Calling it the Friends of the President Golf Day immediately politicises what could simply have been a pleasant day's golf, with a light snack of garlic, beetroot and sweet potato salad at the ninth and a shower in the newly renovated Jacob Zuma Spa and Wellness Centre.

Instead, those who accepted the invitation have been lumped with the sort of people who spend large sums of money to run full-page adverts in newspapers flattering the President in the most embarrassingly syco-phantic way.

I assume that behind all the grovelling obsequiousness the real point of these adverts is to let the President know that a bit of BEE largesse wouldn't go amiss next time there's a juicy deal on the go.

But let's be fair. It's the President's golf day and he can invite whoever he chooses. If I have a party I obviously invite people whose company I enjoy and those I count as friends. But I doubt I would risk scorn by calling the thrash the Friends of David Bullard Party. That smacks of desperation and that's the real problem with the name of the President's golf day; if they were real friends he wouldn't need to remind us of the fact.

One of the ANC's greatest 'friends' was the late Brett Kebble. As we now know it was the sort of friendship that blossoms only when large amounts of stolen money move in unusual ways. Most people's idea of friendship is based on a mutual affection and trust that develops be-tween individuals over years. True friendship is a valuable thing and if you can count your true friends on the fingers of more than one hand then you're very fortunate.

There's nothing wrong with big business and politicians getting to-gether to chew the fat and knock a white ball around in congenial sur-roundings. However, whether all the back-slapping, schmoozing and camaraderie qualifies as friendship is questionable.

Let's be under no illusion; the real aim of the President's golf day is to foster mutually beneficial relationships between politicians who didn't join the struggle to be poor and businessmen with an eye on the bottom line.

ANC's true colours come shining through

3 September 2006

You have to admire the ANC for sticking up for what it really believes in. In a normal society one might have thought that hanging out with a man who is a serial liar and convicted fraudster would be politically career-limiting, but this certainly doesn't seem to be the case in South Africa.

When Tony (Sweaty Hands) Yengeni finally checked into Pollsmoor after his delaying tactics ran out of steam, he was accompanied and cheered on by some of the most powerful members of the ruling party.

Good for them, I say. Just because the ANC's ex-chief whip has been found guilty in court of a criminal offence is no reason to abandon him.

So there was Western Cape Premier Ebrahim Rasool, Speaker of Parliament Baleka Mbete, Housing Minister Lindiwe Sisulu, the President's pet Rottweiler Essop Pahad, and quite a few other 'dignitaries'.

The prison warders obligingly did a dance of welcome for our fallen hero as he arrived in a cavalcade of expensive cars worthy of the banana republic we are fast becoming.

The ANC's fondness for scoundrels and rogues is well known, and if things had been any different we would have smelt a rat. So it is totally appropriate that a political party known for its sleaze and love of all things dubious should honour one of its struggle heroes, even if he is only going to serve a few months of his sentence before being offered another juicy opportunity for self-enrichment at the taxpayer's expense.

Two things occurred to me when I read about this charade. The first is that the legal system in this country is on the brink of collapse and cannot be trusted. Members of the ANC said so themselves and if you can't believe the legislators, who can you believe?

Despite being handed down by a court of law, this verdict is 'a travesty of justice', according to Yengeni. Since no one in the ruling party has disputed the fact, we must assume that the official stance on our legal system is that it cannot be trusted. So if you're dragged off to court you can confidently tell the judge you don't recognise the authority of the court and that you have the backing of the government.

The second thing that occurred to me was how this must look to foreign observers and investors. When people like Pahad constantly champion crooks like Brett Kebble and Yengeni, what signal are we sending out? That's a rhetorical question because it's perfectly obvious: we are telling the rest of the world in the clearest possible language that if you want dealings with South Africa you need to bring something extra to the table.

There are no nudges and winks involved as there are with some countries. Ours is an unequivocal message and it says: 'We're open for business and the dodgier you are, the more we like you.'

Many fellow columnists have fulminated eloquently over the farcical Yengeni imprisonment, but all our words will be lining the hamster's cage within a week. We can protest as much as we like, but nothing is going to change.

The ANC has clearly demonstrated it couldn't give a damn about the rule of law, particularly where chums are concerned. Maybe that's why our rugby is so dire; to distract us from the brand of anarchy the ANC is fomenting.

To vlok or not to vlok, is that the question?

10 September 2006

A new word is about to creep into our rich South African lexicon. The word is 'vlok' and it means to wash the feet of your former enemy. Typical usage would be 'Take off your sandals, I want to vlok you.'

The past tense is obviously 'vlokked' and someone who practices this ancient ritual is known as a 'vlokker', while the recipient of the treatment is the 'vlokee'. I'll let you know when the T-shirt is available.

I have nothing but admiration for the former head of the NP Gestapo's gesture of reconciliation towards the Rev. Frank Chikane, but I couldn't help wondering what you talk about while you're having your feet washed by somebody who once tried to kill you. And I suppose it's not done to comment on the vlokee's bunions and in-grown toenails.

It's bad enough at the hairdresser. My tresses are tended by a delightful Scottish lass, but I soon run out of pleasantries and sit in the chair in dumb silence, desperately trying to think of a topic of conversation that would make me seem interesting to a hairdresser while she snips away.

Things weren't much better when I used to have my hair cut by a traditional English barber. Old-school barbers, unlike hairdressers and hair stylists, are encouraged to learn the art of polite conversation while they practise their tonsorial skills.

However, the conversation tends to stay on safe topics for fear of offending customers. So they'll say something like 'Did you see the match last night, sir?' and then agree with everything you say about the game.

The only way to shut them up is to tell them you didn't see the game. That puts the conversational ball back into the barber's court and he then has to think of another safe topic to broach. I don't think you'll ever hear a barber say: 'I think Iran should nuke somebody just for the hell of it, sir.'

The details are a bit vague on how the vlokking actually came about. Some reports suggest that Adriaan had been pestering Frank for some months by phone, rather like those irritating people who phone me during *3 Talk* offering a special on carpets or wanting to paint my roof at a bargain price because they just happen to be painting roofs in my area that week and have some paint left over.

Others suggest that he just pitched up one day at Frank's office with a bowl and facecloth and told the startled receptionist he wanted to wash the Reverend's feet.

And there's another dilemma. Can you just turn up with a brown plastic washing-up bowl and a bottle of Dettol, or are you expected to vlok your former enemies with something altogether more classy, like a designer Alessi foot-washing bowl with matching soap dish? Will a normal facecloth do, and are you expected to carry a variety of oils and balms for the post-vlok anointing?

I have no doubt that glossy magazines and perhaps even our very own Lifestyle supplement will soon be offering aspirant vlokkers an infallible guide to the whys and wherefores of foot washing, together with a comprehensive list of recommended retail outlets known to stock vlokking paraphernalia.

With any luck the whole thing will fizzle out long before Desmond Tutu comes up with the idea of a mass vlokking of black feet by all those ungrateful whites. Maybe it's easier just to say sorry after all.

Come off it, china, that's not treason

17 September 2006

Maybe it was the hot Dubai sun, or perhaps the glorious sight of so many cranes, but something has obviously happened to our jet-setting Deputy President Phumzile Mlambo-Ngcuka's judgment. To label the importation of cheap Asian garments 'treason' does seem a bit over the top, particularly as some of the government's own Parks Board shops carry souvenirs of South Africa that just happen to be made in China.

The introduction of a quota on clothing items made in China was bound to make retailers seek alternative suppliers, particularly in the run-up to Christmas. The deputy president quite rightly wants to protect South African jobs, but banning the cheap Chinese competition and threatening retailers who naturally want to buy quality goods as cheaply as possible certainly isn't going to achieve that objective.

Our clothing industry is in trouble for one reason alone: we are too expensive. There's nothing wrong with local quality, but we simply cannot compete with China's low labour costs without upsetting the unions.

So what the government has done instead is take choice away from the consumer and put up the price of clothing by insisting we buy South African. My guess is that this attempt at market manipulation will backfire badly and that it will be a Pyrrhic victory for the local clothing and textile industry.

Whether or not the major retailers quake at the deputy president's accusation of treason and stop importing cheap clothing is of no consequence.

The goods will find their way here somehow, and they will be sold at flea markets, at traffic intersections and through the Internet. Their 'Made in China' labels will be removed and 'Proudly made in South Africa' labels sewn in by cheap, non-unionised local labour, and they will gradually make their way back onto the retailer's shelves.

Within a few years we will be buying cars from China at prices that are likely to be substantially less than the traditional competition. Will that also be treason, I wonder, particularly as the government has often called for a cheaper, people's car?

And what about the building industry? Those fancy Italian taps you bought for the bathroom and those designer door handles you want are now made in China at a fraction of the price of the original. Is that treason?

Many of the electrical goods you use every day, including your cellphone, are made in China because large international companies think it's a pretty smart idea to use a cheap labour force and to do business with the government of a country that is determined to dominate world markets, even if it means undercutting other people's prices.

When it comes to buying the latest electrical toy or running shoe, does anyone really care that they are made by sweated labour in China? Well, obviously Zwelinzima Vavi, the general secretary of Cosatu, has to pretend to care but that doesn't stop his main ally, the South African Communist Party, from ordering Chinese-made SACP baseball caps.

Instead of imposing quotas and behaving like a bunch of terminal losers, South Africa would stand a much better chance of being taken seriously if it showed that it could compete for world trade instead of resorting to protectionism.

You mean killer taxis aren't what you want?

24 September 2006

THE delicious irony of taxi drivers complaining that the new 16-seater GAZelle taxi is as unsafe as the decrepit mobile coffins they are supposed to replace will not be lost on readers of this column.

The *Sunday Times* reported last week that 500 Russian GAZelles have been recalled because they suffer from embarrassing flaws such as cracked wheel rims and defective gear levers. The GAZelles are vying for a slice of Comrade Jeff Radebe's R7.7-billion taxi recapitalisation programme.

Gorkovsky Automobilny Zavod (GAZ), or the Gorky Automotive Factory, is the 'the second Russian factory about production' according to one hugely entertaining website devoted to the glories of communist-era motoring.

The company was started in the 1930s and its task was to produce the sort of decadent vehicles Americans enjoyed, with the proviso that the GAZ version could only be enjoyed in Russia by party officials, famous ballet dancers who hadn't defected to the West, and cosmonauts.

Interestingly, the Americans offered technical help when the company was first set up and the early designs were exact replicas of well-known US cars. The US relationship lasted five years and then the Russians were on their own, which allowed them to create some of the most hideous automobiles ever before deciding to ape US car design once again.

Things didn't go terribly well on the mechanical side either, but that didn't matter much in a captive market like the USSR where there was absolutely no choice. One of the prototype models in the '50s proved rather embarrassing because the steering mechanism had obviously been designed by a committee, with the result that the car would turn right if the steering wheel was turned left and vice versa. The plug was pulled on the project and the steering committee almost certainly sent to Siberia.

So GAZ does have a long history of automotive expertise, albeit much of it by trial and error. Which is obviously why the government allowed it to enter the race for the lucrative taxi market ahead of 2010. After all, what more thrilling experience could there be for footie fans than to veer off the road in a Russian-made vehicle and then be relieved of their wallets and cellphones by authentic South Africans?

Some of the more common complaints about the SABS-approved GAZelles are that the windscreens pop out, the dashboards crack and the engines don't work. This is easily explained by the fact that most of the products from GAZ are designed to be driven in a country known to be on the very chilly side for much of the year.

When the same vehicles are transported to a country known to be on the hottish side climatically, then it's hardly surprising things go wrong. This is why reputable motor companies test their products thoroughly in extreme cold and extreme heat. Indeed, South Africa is used by several major motor manufacturers as a test ground for their products.

Of course, the cynics and conspiracy theorists among you will suggest that there is something very fishy about this whole GAZ deal, but I think the explanation is much simpler. GAZ was asked to design a vehicle specifically for the South African market and that it seems to have done by making them as dangerous and unpredictable as the vehicles they replace.

Zuma's goons live in a fool's paradise

8 October 2006

Zuma time and the living is easy. Unless you happen to be gay, in which case things don't look too rosy for you under a Zuma presidency.

And the living might not be quite so easy if you are a critical journalist. Or one of those people involved in the long-running unproven conspiracy to keep Jacob Zuma from the presidency. Or a woman wearing a miniskirt. Or someone dying from Aids.

In fact, the list of those who may well find themselves at the wrong end of Zuma's longed-for machine gun grows by the day.

Now that the fraud case has been chucked out and JZ appears to have taken pole position on the presidential starting grid, the debate concerning his suitability as a future president of this country has a new urgency.

We've already seen the rand tumble against major currencies and it would be naive to suggest that the prospect of a Zuma presidency played no part in that. While there is uncertainty over the ANC succession issue there is bound to be rand volatility.

A recurring theme in the Zuma debate is the suggestion that JZ is not intellectually up to the task of leading the country. His amiable buffoon image may appeal to those who attend his rallies, but it certainly doesn't impress those who believe that a Grade 6 education is inadequate qualification for the world stage.

The Zuma lobby, many of whom regard a Grade 6 education as the

pinnacle of intellectual achievement, argue that the US has a democratically elected idiot for president and what is good for the US should be good
for South Africa. It's a persuasive argument and one that highlights one
of the many flaws in democracy. If you give idiots a vote then they are
quite likely to vote for idiots.

The US may be able to afford the luxury of an idiot president but South
Africa certainly can't.

What we really need is a weighted vote linked to how much tax we
pay. The more you contribute to the country's coffers the more say you
should have in who runs the country.

The system of one man, one vote works only in a society where the
majority are more or less equal. In a country like South Africa, where
the gap between rich and poor is so vast, it takes a great leap of faith to
believe that the majority would vote for anyone on the side of big business.

Since Zuma's ideas on how to run a country are virtually non-existent, his popularity obviously isn't based on future policy. What his supporters seem to relish is the lawlessness of a potential Zuma presidency.
They are whipped up to a frenzy of hatred and violence by Zuma the
rabble rouser, and all the while he beams benignly.

What the rabble don't understand is that they will be dumped by
Zuma and his dubious power elite once they have served their purpose.

We have all been lulled into a false sense of security over the past 12
years. Under the ANC we've enjoyed growth, prosperity and increased
status on the world stage and we have become attractive to foreign investors. We look north to Zimbabwe with pitying eyes and tell ourselves it
couldn't happen here.

Well, my friends, the seeds have already been sown. Just wait for the
harvest.

One old white guy who plans to stay

15 October 2006

Suddenly the newspapers are full of stories about the white exodus and I expect it's only a matter of time before we'll be hoarding baked beans and tins of soup again.

Most of my white friends have glumly taken the view that South Africa holds no future for people with a pale complexion, and have done what all good parents do: educated and prepared their children for lucrative employment opportunities overseas.

Friends in the medical profession have been lamenting the drop in standards for years, and unsubstantiated rumours of exam passes based on quotas for the right skin colour rather than medical knowledge seem all too believable. We should all be worried when being previously disadvantaged because you walked 20 km to school in bare feet gives you a better chance of entering the medical profession than straight As.

One might have thought that taking affirmative action to such ridiculous lengths would deeply offend the many black professionals who have genuinely earned the right to be where they are today.

Fortunately, there are still some who are not afraid to raise their heads above the parapets and tell it like it is. But the majority of black professionals are terrified to rock the boat. How else could we have found ourselves in a situation where we have such a lamentable skills shortage and where people who are completely incapable of doing a job are not only employed but even move on to higher paid employment?

It's a conspiracy of mediocrity and keeping talented whites out reduces the chances of ever being found out. Whistle-blowers like Pascalis
Mokupo should be hailed as national heroes instead of being treated like
lepers. The culture of dishonesty and corruption is now so widespread
that it is people like Mokupo who make the news and not the legion of
crooks all busy making off with a share of the public purse.

Pressure from the government to pretend that black students who
haven't a hope of passing exams should still be allowed to practise as
doctors will eventually devalue academic institutions. So is it any wonder that parents are prepared to make huge financial sacrifices just so
their children can get a credible qualification at a proper teaching estab-
lishment?

The high levels of dangerous crime are also given as a reason for white
emigration, but that has always been a factor in this country; part of
the risk-reward ratio, if you like. My guess is that whites would be more
prepared to put up with the appalling crime levels if they felt their skills
were appreciated and would be rewarded. But most of the job adverts
in our brave new non-racial world make it quite clear that it would be
pointless for whites to apply.

So am I about to leave?

Not a chance. As this newspaper's resident middle-aged white polemi-
cist, I have to keep the flag flying.

Besides, my neighbour has just introduced various amphibians to his
garden pond and I am serenaded to sleep every night by the deep croak
of the Red Toad and woken in the morning by the hadeda ibis. Does life
get better than that?

Bring back the rope, starve the prisoners

22 October 2006

Isn't it time we had a national referendum on the re-introduction of the death penalty? I'm not sure matters of such importance should be left to the Constitutional Court – it puts too heavy a burden on the learned judges' shoulders.

The people should be allowed to decide, and my guess is that the vote would go overwhelmingly in favour of the death penalty.

In fact, I would suggest that if you asked the great South African public if they would be in favour of public executions they would tick the Yes box. The majority of decent people are so fed up with violent crime that they would do anything to be rid of it, and watching convicted criminals dangle from a rope or fry in an electric chair might help the healing process.

The argument that there is no place for the death penalty in a civilised society is completely irrelevant in this country. We are not a civilised society. We are a cowering society brutalised by violent criminals who have weighed the risks against the rewards and sensibly decided that crime pays magnificently in South Africa, particularly when one has an impotent, bickering government unwilling to tackle real problems for fear of alienating its voters.

Criminals violate other people's rights, and yet we insist that theirs should be respected as if they were naughty children who had pinched an extra slice of chocolate cake.

This is madness. Criminals, and especially violent criminals, deserve no rights. They gave them up voluntarily when they decided on a life of crime. Prison should be a dreadful experience, not a rehabilitation centre.

When and if we approach civilisation, maybe that can change, but until then the prospect of a prison sentence should fill would-be crooks with dread.

Does the government pay your grocery bill? Does it drop off food parcels at your home? Of course it doesn't, so why are we supplying people who have offended society with free food? If you are sentenced to prison, the responsibility to feed you should belong to your family. If they don't turn up with food or the money for food, then bad luck, you starve to death just as you would in the free world.

Then there's the lengthy wait for justice to be dispensed, which usually affords the arrested criminals plenty of time to escape from custody while they are waiting for their day in court. If the police turn up at the scene of a violent crime, why the hell aren't they allowed to shoot the bastards? That way justice is effectively dispensed and the court's time isn't wasted. It would motivate the police and would certainly act as a deterrent to the criminals, who would suddenly have to factor in a real risk when planning their criminal endeavours.

The swift execution of violent criminals would certainly go some way to convincing the majority of law-abiding citizens that the government was serious about cracking down on crime. It might even make those considering a life of crime think twice.

Convincing ourselves that it's all society's fault and there wouldn't be crime without poverty is a pathetic cop-out. Weeding out society's antisocial misfits and sending them to the death chamber is a much more sensible option if you want to sleep easy at night.

Not much new out of Africa, Madonna

29 October 2006

On the wall of the Portrait Gallery in Edinburgh hangs a painting of a titled gentleman of the 19th century. To his right stands a small black boy with a metal collar around his neck. The note on the wall beside the painting explains that it was common at the time to keep black children as slaves.

Owning a black child was a sign of your standing within the community, a status symbol. The note went on to explain that when the children grew up they were usually shipped back to the West Indies, where they died of hunger or disease. No doubt the ship dropping off the 'past its cute date' slave would pick up a new batch of adorable wide-eyed black babies for the English nobility.

Major Grant, founder of the famous distillery that makes Glen Grant, had a black servant. The major enjoyed hunting in India and Africa, and on one trip to Africa saw two boys standing by the roadside. He gave chase; one escaped, but the other was caught by the major, who brought him back to a chilly Scotland as a curiosity and a future servant. One can only wonder what happened at customs as the major brought his luggage through the green channel.

'Morning, Major, welcome back tae Scotland. Have ye anything tae declare? Hang aboot. What's that thing wriggling in yer bag?'

'Och, it's just a wee dark laddie I caught in Africa. Can I keep him? Oh please can I, can I?'

'Well, strictly speaking, Major, you should nae be bringing in wee darkies, but as it's you I'll turn a blind eye this time.'

So Madonna is doing nothing new. The sad fact is that we haven't really progressed in nearly 200 years.

For some reason, black children are much more adorable than white children. Given the choice of a wide-eyed, starving black urchin with flies all over his face, or a snotty-nosed Chechen kid in what remains of his bombed home, our hearts go out to the black kid every time. I wouldn't be in the least bit surprised if one of the major toy companies rushed out a David Banda doll in time for Christmas.

Many people will argue that life with Mr and Mrs Ritchie in one of their splendid homes, a R75 000 rocking horse in the new nursery (painted out as a jungle, if you please) and unlimited access to recreational drugs is a much more attractive proposition than growing up poor in rural Malawi.

That rather depends on whether you believe money is the cure for all ills.

My own view is that young David is about to embark on the most horrific life journey. His adoptive mother cares so much about him that she flew out separately and entrusted him to a paid nanny on a scheduled airline. When he arrived the following morning, she was out at gym and David quickly became just another of Madonna's fashion accessories.

Will she still love him when he's no longer cute and wide-eyed, or will he be flown back to Malawi and swapped for the latest model?

Only time will tell. But one thing we can be sure of: this is no act of pop star philanthropy; it's just another in a long line of Madonna's cheap publicity stunts. And you don't get much cheaper than poor black African babies.

Death to scum is a democratic choice

5 November 2006

I wasn't at all surprised to read in last week's *Sunday Times* that the majority of South Africans, black and white, support a referendum on the death penalty, with 69% of those polled saying they would vote to bring back the death penalty. The reader response to a column I wrote on the subject two weeks ago was overwhelmingly supportive of the reintroduction of the death penalty.

However, I was surprised at the reaction from the ivory-tower experts. David Bruce of the Centre for the Study of Violence and Reconciliation reckons it would be a step backwards for the state to become a 'machinery of death'. He says 'it would be the same people who have been brutalised through systemic violence in the past and who still suffer because of inequity and the legacy of racism who would bear the brunt if the death penalty is reinstated'. Which is a long-winded way of saying lots of black people would be hanged.

Yet, 72% of blacks want a referendum on the death penalty. And I suspect the state's 'machinery of death' would be rather more merciful than the criminals' machinery of death, but Bruce clearly disagrees.

Peter Gastrow, Cape Town director of the Institute for Security Studies, reckons that allowing people to vote for the death penalty would be a big mistake because it would open the door for other populist and emotional issues such as land distribution to be put before the nation. So if we hang murderers we might have to start giving people land. I'm not too sure I follow the logic of that argument.

Finally, Barbara Holtmann, the project manager of the Crime-Prevention Centre at the Centre for Scientific and Industrial Research, reckons the death penalty is the most appalling response; 'to say we will kill people because we're angry with them. People may call for it but are they prepared to be hangmen?'

Despite her fancy job title, one can't help wondering if Holtmann fully understands the issue. We're not killing people because we're angry with them; that's what road rage is for. We're proposing to kill them because a court of law has found them to be antisocial scumbags with no regard for human life.

And if you're looking for a hangman, you know where to get hold of me.

While Bruce, Gastrow and Holtmann are quite entitled to their views, two things scare me about their comments. The first is that they all work for what appear to be quasi-government boondoggles and yet seem hideously out of touch with the feelings of the people who are paying their salaries. The second is the rather patronising tone of their responses. They seem to be telling us that the hoi polloi can't be expected to understand the complexity of the debate because we are emotionally unstable. Let the experts decide what is best for us. Well, if that really is the case then we no longer have democracy.

I would love to live in the sort of civilised society where there is no place for the death penalty, but I don't. I live in one of the most violent countries in the world. I've got more chance of being killed here than I have in a war zone. I'm fed up and so are 76.5% of my countrymen, so can we please have that referendum as soon as possible.

A mild life is better than no life at all

12 November 2006

O n a recent visit to the UK, I turned on the TV in my hotel room just in time to catch one of those mini-documentaries about the strange habits of weird South Africans. This one was about the bizarre cult of train surfing: an activity that involves running along the roof of a moving railway carriage while trying to avoid getting electrocuted by the overhead cables.

It sounds like a pretty daft thing to do but, as the programme made clear, if you're dirt poor, live in a squalid township and have absolutely no hope of ever getting a job, this is probably the most excitement that life has to offer.

Train surfers were interviewed and asked if they weren't put off by the fact that their friends often ended up as sizzling corpses lying by a railway track. They weren't. Train surfing was dangerous but cool. It was a way of standing out from the common herd; of becoming a local celebrity if you survived, or a statistic if you didn't.

Even if you don't die, running along the roof of a moving railway carriage is a pretty good way of eventually sustaining a serious injury, but that doesn't seem to put the train surfers off. For them it's a win-win situation. If they climb down in one piece they will be heroes and if they tangle with the overhead cables they will die a noble death and be spared the futility of their lives.

Does the same perverse logic apply to the use of seat belts, I wonder?

I can't imagine getting into a car and not putting my seat belt on, but maybe that's because I have a vivid imagination and some knowledge of Newton's first law of motion. Similarly, I wouldn't attempt to take a casserole dish out of a hot oven without first putting on an oven glove, and I would prefer to disconnect the electricity supply before unscrewing and changing a light switch.

Maybe I'm just a wimp. Cricketers now dress in all sorts of protective armour and it would be unthinkable for a wicketkeeper to turn up in a sun hat and without all the usual visible bodily protection. If there's a way of protecting yourself against possible injury, it just seems crazy not to use it.

Tragically, the recent deaths of two prominent South Africans has focused attention on the use of seat belts. Both victims were thrown clear from the vehicles and, as it's virtually impossible to be thrown from a car if you're wearing a seat belt, it suggests belts weren't being worn.

A recent newspaper article suggested that wearing a seat belt is not considered cool in certain sectors. Presumably being laid out on a morgue slab is way cooler.

I've often stopped next to cars where young children are standing up in the back between the driver and the passenger's seat or kneeling on the rear seat looking out of the rear window. I used to wind down my window and politely tell the driver to please strap their child in, but that sort of caring behaviour on my part generally resulted in a vile stream of execration so I've given up. I now sit calmly in my car and rationalise that if idiot parents want to kill themselves and their children it's obviously no business of mine and, besides, by eliminating themselves they deepen the gene pool and do us all a huge favour. The last thing we need is more idiots reproducing.

Wanted: a backbone and decisive action

19 November 2006

There is absolutely no shame in being an invertebrate. If you're a worm, a sponge, an insect or a slug then being spineless is a positive advantage, particularly when it comes to getting around nimbly and finding food.

Admittedly there is a downside. If you're a mollusc it's often difficult to differentiate your head from your anus, but that can also work to your advantage – as some of our political invertebrates have found out recently. I have thus far refrained from making any comment about the head of the SABC for fear of being labelled a liberal intent on hijacking our democratic values of ubuntu. You all know how I hate being called a liberal.

However, the term 'political invertebrate' could just as easily be applied to Dali Mpofu as it could to the obsequious vassals responsible for bringing us their anodyne version of the news. Mpofu recently had the perfect opportunity to put things right at the state-owned broadcaster, but he wimped out, played safe and brown-nosed his political paymasters.

A far more sinister example of spinelessness is the appalling handling of the Jackie Selebi affair. As if he hasn't enough on his plate already, our poor beleaguered Police Commissioner is accused of keeping the company of dodgy people who engage in drug dealing and money laundering and of receiving kickbacks and perverting the course of justice.

These wild allegations have been blowing around for some months now and there are only two conclusions to be drawn. If they are false then we should be very worried that a man seen fit by the international community to head Interpol should be subjected to such a vicious character assassination. If they are true then we should be even more worried and should be notifying Fifa that we won't be holding the 2010 World Cup here because we are not worthy.

At the moment, though, these are just allegations and the problem is that the political invertebrates have done absolutely nothing to either dispel the rumours or to set a proper investigation in motion. So we live with the surreal situation of our top cop being accused of the most dreadful things while the nation and the world are left to speculate as to whether there is even a semblance of truth in the accusations. Selebi may not have enjoyed much success in bringing down violent crime in this country, but that's hardly good reason to accuse him of being a kingpin in a major crime syndicate.

President Thabo Mbeki is not a man known for swift action, but vacillation on this issue really isn't an option. Instead of the usual invertebrate response, which involves the government doing sod all and hoping the whole thing blows over, he urgently needs to appoint an impartial (that is, non-ANC aligned) commission of inquiry made up of reliable senior police officers from the international community to clear this matter up once and for all.

The South African Police Service cannot function efficiently while doubt lingers over its commander-in-chief. More importantly, though, Mbeki owes it to the long-suffering South African taxpayer for whom being a victim of violent crime is now more a matter of when rather than if.

'Racist' tag is my badge of honour

26 November 2006

If you're the sort of person who thinks the Gaza Strip is the name of a lap-dancing joint somewhere in the Middle East and that Camp David is a gay friend of the US president, then you probably won't be too worried about the frightening level of corruption within the ruling party.

The economic miracle that has been cleverly engineered to take your mind off the thieving and grand larceny will probably do exactly what it was intended to do: make you feel good and not ask too many impertinent questions.

For those of us who aren't fooled by all the smoke and mirrors, things are not quite so rosy. Every day brings reports of ever more horrific stories of senior political or business figures with their hands deep in the cookie jar.

Those who have been caught, prosecuted and imprisoned treat the whole thing as a huge joke and give the rest of us the finger from behind prison walls, knowing that their corrupt buddies will see them right.

Those not actively involved in rigging tenders, setting up dubious nominee companies, employing unqualified family members or just helping themselves to public money are involved in some other scandal. They're either linked to shady business characters or reclining on a bed, asking a young woman to fondle their genitals.

We appear to live in a society where only the most venal and dishonest survive and prosper.

But there is hope. A growing number of eloquent black commentators are voicing their disgust at the ANC's apparent disregard for democratic accountability and its squandering of the hard-won freedom of 1994.

I am frequently referred to in hate mail as a racist. I suppose it doesn't help that I have a white skin and carry the passport of a former colonial oppressor.

However, these days I regard the accusation of racism as a badge of honour. It suggests that something I have written is upsetting someone in a position of power.

For the past 12 years the ANC has gone out of its way to discredit its critics by accusing them of racism. Even the President had an unfortunately timed go at whiteys who perpetuate the image of the black man who can't control his sexual urges.

While it was mostly whites who were doing the criticising, it was a successful ploy because it effectively gagged most of white business, who were too terrified to stand up against political corruption for fear of being labelled racist.

Then there was the added threat of affirmative action, which is nothing more than a form of economic ethnic cleansing. Whites were obviously too frightened to speak out, in case they lost their jobs.

So a combination of political deviousness and psychological bullying, accompanied by a cavalier attitude towards the very people they purport to represent, has allowed the corrupt and incompetent to flourish in our society.

Since the 'racism' smear has become somewhat devalued over the years, I do hope that those I criticise in this column will stop using it. If I tell you that you are a dishonest, utterly useless #@$$*, then please take it at face value and believe me when I tell you that you would still qualify for the insult whatever your skin colour.

That's true equality for you.

Putting the 'mock' into democracy

3 December 2007

Over the past few weeks, pretty well every magazine and newspaper I have read has contained an editorial or a column suggesting that there are too many question marks hanging over Police Commissioner Jackie Selebi's head for him to continue in the job.

The cartoonists have repeatedly shown him in an unflattering light and the callers to the talk radio shows I have listened to have said that his name needs to be cleared if we are to have any confidence in the South African Police Service.

The message from the people could not have been clearer, yet the Cabinet voted to take no action, either to clear Selebi's name or to investigate the very serious accusations against him.

The government will predictably argue that the authors of articles in newspapers and the sort of people who phone in to radio stations are not representative of the demographics of the country (although they are probably representative of the bulk of the taxes collected) but they are deluding themselves.

The mood of the country is changing and the people are sending very clear messages to President Thabo Mbeki that they are heartily sick of the antics of his menagerie of bunglers, rip-off artists and seasoned liars who are all too busy enriching themselves to care.

We must, of course, remember that they didn't join the struggle to be poor (© Smuts Ngonyama).

The government raises its collective middle finger to us with such frequency these days that I've decided to coin a new word to describe the South African system of government: demockracy.

It has all the essential hallmarks of democracy in that elections are held once every five years, but in the intervening years it renders the electorate helpless while they watch in stunned amazement as their elected representatives line their pockets and mock the people by carrying convicted sleaze-bags to prison on their shoulders, suggest that vegetables can cure Aids, have sex with unwilling young women because they are dressed provocatively, tell those complaining of crime to leave the country, accept generous gifts from dishonest mining magnates and so on and so forth ad nauseam.

When we first heard of government corruption, we experienced a feeling of disappointment but rationalised that we were a new democracy and there were bound to be a few bad eggs. We were prepared to believe that the good politicians outnumbered the bad.

Then, as the cancer of corruption spread and it became obvious that senior members of the ANC had no interest in accountability, our disappointment grew into despair as we realised that the only thing that had really changed in South Africa was the names of the robber barons.

That despair has now moved into the anger stage; anger that we could have been so gullible and anger that those accused get way with it time and time again.

The next stage, if the fate of other highly corrupt governments is anything to go by, will probably be violent uprising as the people of South Africa come to realise that the only way forward is to remove the cancer completely.

But the politicians know that already, don't they? Why do you think they will only venture out in public if they are surrounded by a phalanx of armed bodyguards?

Fine to wine, but remember the profits

10 December 2006

A few weeks ago a new wine found its way on to the exclusive shelves of Johannesburg's premier wine retailer and on to the wine lists of a few select restaurants.

The wine is the much-anticipated David Bullard Out to Lunch White (a zesty, eloquent white wine) and the Out to Lunch Red (PC wine made from black grapes), both available at a ridiculously cheap R40 a bottle.

Now this may look like a shameless product punt to you, but stay with me because there is a purpose to this story.

Although it bears my name and the name of this column on the label, I had absolutely nothing to do with the making, blending, bottling, label design or distribution of this wine. I get much of the credit of course and many people will now assume that I own a wine estate but, in truth, I haven't had to risk a cent of my own money.

All the hard work was done by the dapper Ken Forrester. He bought the farm and grew the grapes. It was his fermentation tanks that made the wine, he blended it, bottled it and brought it to market. Despite all this hard work his name appears in very small writing on the side of the label, while I get the kudos.

The fact that he's made a very quaffable couple of wines obviously pleases me, but the obvious question to be asked is this: Why does a well-known winemaker like Ken Forrester need me? And why does a well-known construction company need a handful of opportunistic politicians to help them build the Gautrain?

I have already speculated in previous columns that the real purpose of the Gautrain is not to get people to the airport quickly or to ease road congestion but to enrich a group of cronies. The cost of the project will billow well beyond budgeted costs and a handful of well-connected folk will be buying bits of the Cape coastline on their ill-gotten gains.

It's the arms deal scandal all over again except that a new transport system is the equivalent of protected royal game. If we attack the idea we'll obviously be accused of not wanting black people to be able to travel in comfort. So best we just shut up and fume instead.

In old-style capitalism there were only two reasons to belong to a consortium to build something like the Gautrain. The first was that you came to the party with a thick wad of money and became an investor. The second was that you brought some specialised engineering skills to the project for which you would be rewarded.

So what particular engineering skills do members of the government bring to the Gautrain project? Do any of the Bombela consortium names mentioned in the press have experience of building railways? I doubt it. So they must be bringing money to the table, mustn't they?

But that can't be right either because, if the ANC is to be believed, black people never had the opportunity to accumulate wealth in the old South Africa.

So the only conclusion one can come to is that political influence has been peddled in return for a cut of the construction profits. Even a miniscule cut of a R23-billion taxpayer-funded project is worth banking.

I'm planning to give my share of the profits on the Out to Lunch wines to charity, mainly because I feel I haven't earned them. I wonder if any Bombela beneficiaries would like to follow my example?

Beastly despots live the longest

17 December 2007

Too much fatty food will clog your arteries and lead to a heart attack, smoking kills and unprotected sex is a complete no-no (unless you shower immediately afterwards).

Add to that the possibility that some thug sprung from C-Max by corrupt Correctional Services employees could gun you down in your driveway and you realise that staying alive is damn difficult.

It seems the only guarantee of longevity is to become a dictator. Slaughter thousands of your citizens or, better still, make them simply disappear off the face of the earth and you will live to a ripe old age.

Bring your country to its knees economically and stash the money you've stolen in a foreign bank account and you will be blessed with the rudest of health.

Torture your political enemies and indulge in a spot of genocide and you can be sure you'll still be around to take advantage of your pensioner's bus pass.

Augusto Pinochet, the Chilean dictator, has just snuffed it at the grand old age of 91.

Although widely regarded by his political opponents and the families of his victims as a monster and, despite being described by the Chilean novelist Isabel Allende as 'a byword for brutality and ignorance', he still managed to clock up his four score years and 10.

That is no mean feat for someone who, one might have thought, had irritated enough people in his life to find himself in the cross-hairs of an assassin's rifle sight. For some reason this never seems to happen, though.

Run through the list of modern tyrants and dictators and you'll find that many enjoy a long and healthy life. PW Botha died at 90, Mad Bob is still showing no sign of becoming any less obnoxious in his 80s and while Saddam Hussein may no longer be in power he will reach the age of 70 next year, which is more than can be said for many of his newly liberated countrymen.

Juan Peron was 79 when he died, Joseph Stalin 74 and even Romania's Nicolae Ceausescu made it to the grand old age of 71 before the people had the brilliant idea of shooting him and his wife on Christmas Day in 1989.

Mao Zedong popped his clogs at 82 and while Fidel Castro may not be dancing the rumba these days he has managed to hold out to age 80, which isn't bad for a cigar smoker.

I could go on but you get my drift.

The obvious philosophical question is: How can a merciful deity allow such brutes to live for so long?

Well, maybe he/she isn't as merciful as we like to believe or maybe he/she just has a very sick sense of humour.

The rather more practical question is: What are the dictators doing right that the rest of us are doing wrong?

Why do perfectly decent people become ill and die at a young age while the rotters seem to go on for ever?

Although medical science has yet to confirm it, I'm convinced that being really beastly to your fellow men must increase your resistance to all sorts of life-threatening diseases.

Some of you may take a glass or two of red wine a day in the hope of keeping your arteries clear of blockages or cut down on salt to avoid a stroke. What you should probably be doing is testing your new nerve gas on the people in the next suburb.

It was the year to get loaded

24 December 2006

The end of the year is traditionally a time of personal reflection. We look back on the previous 12 months and ask whether it's been a good year for us. The obvious measure is whether you're financially better off now than you were 12 months ago. Which is probably why 32 million South Africans never bother to review the year; they already know the answer.

For the rest of us, it is a vitally important question. Since the whole purpose of life is to amass as much money as possible and own lots of homes, flat-screen TVs and fast cars, it makes sense for us to do a year-end tally.

To put it bluntly, if you haven't made it in 2006, you're never going to make it.

Judging by the spending, it's been a bonanza year. I'm not talking about the increased value of your house and unit trusts either. That falls under the category of involuntary wealth creation. If you had a house or unit trusts you couldn't help but make money, and that's no credit to you.

No, what I'm talking about are the extra helpings of moolah that have been so liberally doled out this year; the fat bonuses, the share options, the private-equity deal profits and all that BEE largesse. The sort of silly money that allows you to order the best there is without worrying about the cost.

The other day I asked a man at a bar I frequent why he was putting Coke into his Johnnie Walker Blue Label. 'Because I can afford to,' he said. If you drink a premium brand like that, at between R3 000 and R5 000 a bottle, you make sure the waiter leaves it on the table for all to see.

When retailers in the malls of Johannesburg's northern suburbs describe the spending as 'sickening' then you have to sit up and take notice. Not that they're complaining about the sales. Far from it. What they're complaining about it the quality of shopper. It's all about conspicuous consumption; being seen to be spending.

Conspicuous consumption is now so in that Thrupps, the top-people's grocer, has installed screens which face the customer at every checkout. It will probably say this is to help clients check the tally as the cashier swipes the groceries through the bar-code machine. Actually, it's to show the people just behind you in the queue not only what you're buying but how much you're spending.

I've always thought Pick 'n Pay should have a rich-bastards' checkout with a huge TV screen above it that displays your extravagance for all to see. Rather like with the scoring of a century at the Wanderers, there would be a polite ripple of applause from other shoppers as your bill hits five figures.

As Gordon Gekko said in the movie *Wall Street*, 'Greed is good.' Even President Thabo Mbeki agrees with that. Admittedly he didn't earlier this year, but now he has to, probably because he's surrounded by so many greedy colleagues. How much is enough is not a question anyone on the political gravy train stops to ask any more than they wonder about the morality of pretending to be concerned for the poor while helping themselves to the sort of money businessmen used to spend a lifetime accumulating.

In the late '80s, the British comedian Harry Enfield invented a grotesque character called Loadsamoney. All he could talk about was how much money he was making. As so often happens, life imitated art and soon the UK was full of real-life Loadsamoneys. It takes the colonies a while to catch up but catch up we eventually do and we now have our very own Loadsamoneys. They've got the latest cellphone, drive cars so powerful they can barely control them and wear labels rather than clothes.

Believe it or not, there really are people who think there's nothing obscene about blowing R96 000 on lunch or R4.5 million on a jaunt to the UK ... particularly if it's somebody else's money.

The reason old money doesn't flaunt itself is probably because it knows how difficult it was to make the money in the first place. It's a very different matter when you suddenly discover you have shares worth R100 million and no idea how you made the money. The obvious reaction is to spend it as quickly as possible just in case you wake up to find you're dreaming.

That doesn't really explain all the flashiness, though. It is possible to buy life's luxuries without anyone knowing about it, but that's not the South African way. We're an insecure lot and lavish, showy spending is the only way many people have of making the rest of us think they are doing well. Driving the right car suggests that you're successful, even if your workmates regard you as a complete incompetent.

So we've created a monster and, for once, it really is the fault of the media. People beg to be featured on our social pages and the high rollers love it when their spending habits are detailed in other sections of the newspaper.

What used to be an embarrassing invasion of personal privacy is now a badge of honour. You know you're in trouble when Paris Hilton looks classy compared to some of the people who appear on the social pages.

HAVE YOU MADE THE GRADE IN 2006?

1. Are you rude to waiters?
2. Do you order expensive liquor by the bottle and leave it on the table for everyone to see?
3. Do you park your new SUV in the disabled parking spot because it's nearer the ATM?

4. When the bill is presented at the end of the evening, do you hand over a wad of R200 notes and ask: 'Is that enough?'
5. Do you have a cellphone with television reception?
6. Are your shoes handmade?
7. Has Ferrari begged you to buy an Enzo?
8. Do you have a private jet to lend the deputy president?
9. Do you employ more than three domestic workers per home?
10. Are you being sued by Jacob Zuma?

Score 1 point each if the answer is yes to questions 1–9. Score a massive 10 points if the answer is yes to question 10.

On vacation with the hoi polloi

7 January 2007

Like most other wealthy Johannesburg residents, in late November I write the name of the location of all the holiday homes I can recall owning on a small piece of paper. Then I scrunch all the bits of paper into tight balls and drop them into a glass bowl. What usually happens at this stage is that we pick a ball of paper, open it up, read the name of the location of the property, and that's the house we spend our Christmas holiday in.

It couldn't be simpler. Except for this year. The first ball of paper we opened suggested that we should be heading off to our mansion in Plettenberg Bay. Unfortunately, I'd forgotten (as one does when one is a multiple home-owner) that I had sold the house to a Nigerian drug dealer a few months earlier, so we had to draw again. The second ball suggested Kenton-On-Sea, and we'd almost booked our flights when my wife reminded me that we demolished the house back in May and were still busy building an even bigger one to obstruct Matthew Lester's sea view. I'm never quite sure why we bought in Kenton in the first place. The novelty of having no water soon wore off, but it seemed fairly inexpensive compared with some other coastal locations and as I had a few million rands doing nothing in particular at the time, I decided to buy a house there just so that I could knock it down.

With Plett and Kenton out of the running, we were down to only three possibilities. The Cape Town flat would have been perfect but we had let it at R25 000 a day to a couple of celebrity cocaine addicts. Which left the game farm and the cave in Tora Bora, which we bought on spec from a nice American gentleman a few years back. We're still waiting for electricity to be installed, so it wouldn't have been the ideal venue to roast a turkey, which meant that we would have to go to the game farm, but we decided it would be too hot at this time of year.

So, through no real fault of our own, we were forced to spend the Christmas holiday in Johannesburg and what a horrific experience it proved to be. The weather was rubbish and most of the decent restaurants were closed, with the result that places like Parkhurst looked like one of those 'morning after the atomic bomb' movies.

The only good thing about Johannesburg at this time of year is that there's less traffic, but any euphoria you might feel about being able to finally floor the gas pedal on the William Nicol highway disappears when you see a Metro cop crouching in the bushes with a speed trap.

However, the worst thing about being in Johannesburg over the Christmas holiday is the shame of having to venture out to the shops for food after the big day itself. Your mere presence in a shopping mall on 27 December marks you as one of life's also-rans. You may as well be wearing a T-shirt with the words 'I can't afford a holiday home.'

It's not surprising the stores have sales in early January, because the sort of people they attract can barely afford the parking at somewhere like Sandton City. At this time of year you even get people from places like Bedfordview visiting the northern suburbs malls just to get a glimpse of how the rich live.

Fortunately, they blend in with the single-residence flotsam and jetsam of the northern suburbs; the sort of people who would have been living in Bedfordview had their wealthy parents not lent them the money for a home in Parkview.

A welcome oasis in desert of graft

14 January 2007

The position of ANC chief whip is a remnant of the old Westminster system. This will probably come as surprising news to those politicians who thought they had freed themselves from their colonial shackles. The job of the chief whip is to ensure party discipline and to facilitate communication between the back benches and the Cabinet; particularly important when the back benchers' views are not in accord with their party leaders.

The name 'whip' is borrowed, appropriately enough, from another blood sport. In fox hunting the 'whipper in' has the job of making sure the hounds don't straggle but remain as a pack. The obvious analogy between the hunting field and party politics meant that the position was also known as 'whipper in' when originally used in a political context and was later shortened to 'whip'. Obviously anyone holding the very important position of chief whip needs to demonstrate a high level of integrity and be beyond reproach.

The ANC hasn't been very successful with their past two chief whips. One is currently on a short holiday at the taxpayer's expense at the Malmesbury Spa and Wellness Centre after being found guilty of fraud, and the other has been sacked for being a dirty old man.

Tony (Sweaty Palms) Yengeni is due to be released on parole soon and I wouldn't be surprised if the same bunch of dissemblers who carried their hero to prison last year are not there to greet him with a convoy of expensive automotive bling. No doubt a cushy and well-paid job will be found for Sweaty Palms on condition that he keeps his picture out of the newspapers for a month or two.

Mbulelo Goniwe hasn't been quite so lucky though. At a disciplinary hearing last year the old skirt-lifter was sent into the political wilderness for three years and stripped of his office. I must say that this came as something of a shock to me, albeit a welcome shock. For years the ANC has been the party of 'lie and deny'. With the exception of the sacking of Jacob Zuma, the ruling party seems to exhibit a high tolerance level when it comes to dishonesty and corruption.

For example, the Travelgate crooks may have been fingered long ago but they still have their jobs. Does Goniwe's sacking mean that the ANC is finally about to take internal party discipline seriously or was it just a flash in the pan?

Much as I would like to believe that the Goniwe hearing is a sign that the ANC has finally decided to clean up its act, I fear that the popping of champagne corks may be premature. What always puzzles me is that the ANC has some very honourable and hard-working people among its senior members and yet we never hear a peep out of them. Surely somebody has the guts to stand up and state that the party of liberation lost its way long ago and urgently needs a morality makeover. Perhaps the festering corruption within the ANC has become so bad that it is simply too dangerous to voice one's opinion in public.

Fortunately, there is a credible voice of reason. My old adversary Professor Barney Pityana (he once tried to drag me before the Human Rights Commission on charges of racism) came over very well on the BBC's *Hard Talk* programme this week.

At the time of writing the ANC was still desperately casting about for a new chief whip. Look no further; Pityana's your man.

Come on JZ, sue me, I'm waiting

21 January 2007

Last July I received a letter from Mr Wycliffe Thipe Mothuloe B.Iuris LLB (Natal) LLM (UP). Mr Mothuloe represents Mr Jacob Zuma and sent me two letters demanding payment of damages arising from injurious and defamatory articles written by me and published by the *Sunday Times*.

The amount of damages claimed came to a total of R6 million, which was supposed to be paid by 17 July 2006. Naturally I didn't send Mothuloe a cheque, partly because the amount claimed was so derisory as to be insulting (he claimed R15 million from my colleague Zapiro), but mainly because I didn't have a spare six million kicking around at the time. Even if I had, I don't think I would have been disposed to give it to Zuma.

The final sentence of the letter from Mothuloe warned that, should the boodle not be forthcoming, his client would institute legal action to claim the said amount from me. It's now almost February 2007 and I'm becoming a bit bored by the whole process.

My life has been on hold since 17 July 2006. For six months I have had to turn down overseas car launches, invitations to the Golden Globe Awards, parties at the Playboy mansion and a visit to last year's new Ring at the Wagner festival in Bayreuth just in case I had to appear in court to defend press freedom against JZ.

My international legal team has been on red alert for six months and top libel QCs from the Inner Temple don't come cheaply. They've been hanging around in chambers, twiddling their thumbs, turning down other lucrative briefs and biding their time in El Vinos awaiting my call. I'm embarrassed. My life needs to move on. As the Americans say, I need closure.

Since I anticipate spending a large part of the coming year out of the country at various exotic locations, I need to get the tedious business of litigation out of the way as soon as possible. At least the six-month interval has given me a chance to move my global assets into a web of untouchable trust funds so when I stand up in court I can now honestly claim to be a man of straw.

Not that this should bother JZ. He commented recently that his spat with the media wasn't about the money. Since he's suing a group of us for more than R60 million this may come as a surprise, but it is a comment that could affect the eventual outcome of the case if it ever comes to court.

JZ wants to sue the South African media as a matter of principle and for that he should be applauded. Principles haven't been JZ's strong point in the past so it's heartwarming to see that he now recognises such things exist.

So, since he's not interested in the money, a judge could easily find in favour of JZ and award punitive damages in the amount of R1 with each side to pay their own costs. That would satisfy JZ's honour but might leave him a bit out of pocket when it comes to paying his legal team. Oh sorry, I forgot, they are apparently acting pro bono.

Since there is an important constitutional and legal principle at stake here (not to mention my reputation as a columnist) I would strongly urge JZ to pull his finger out and sue us all as he threatened back in July. In the past he has demanded his day in court. Now I demand mine.

Besides, how can you ever again trust the word of a presidential hopeful who promises to sue the media and then fails to do so?

Not so sweet to be an idiot on TV

28 January 2007

Just when it looked as though Herschelle Gibbs's remarks about badly behaved Pakistani cricket supporters might cause a major international incident, the situation was saved by someone called Jade Goody.

In case you haven't been following the story, the porcine-featured Goody was appearing in the UK version of the TV programme *Big Brother*, where she made racist remarks about a fellow inmate, who happens to be a stunning-looking Indian actress called Shilpa Shetty.

In a way the incidents are similar. Gibbs was recorded by a hidden microphone and Goody was filmed by a hidden camera.

The difference is that Gibbs would have no reason to think that his private comments to his teammates were being eavesdropped upon by a cricket stump, whereas Goody knew very well that the cameras were rolling.

That, after all, is the whole point of reality television. So Gibbs's minor indiscretion was booted off the front pages to make way for Goody's ugly racist rant.

Goody was voted out of the *Big Brother* house just over a week ago and only then did she become aware of the massive public outcry and the fact that her antics had been discussed in Parliament and had made international headlines.

There was even talk of her being prosecuted under English law for hate speech and, since the evidence has been seen by millions of people already, it wouldn't be a difficult case to prove.

Predictably, she rapidly issued some apologies and denials and then blubbed on television, which really wasn't a pretty sight.

It may be that she was crying because she was genuinely sorry for her behaviour, but it seems more probable that she was bawling her eyes out because her days as a 'celebrity' are limited and the money is about to stop flowing.

Mediocrity is a feature of Tony Blair's Britain, where the lowest common denominator is revered.

Goody may rightly be accused of making derogatory remarks about Indians, but she is a victim of something far worse, which I will call, for want of a better name, 'moronism'.

Now that fox hunting has been banned, the new sport in England is to send people from a TV station on to the streets to find the stupidest person imaginable and then put them on TV to be mocked by the rest of us. Poor Goody fitted the bill perfectly. She's overweight and unattractive, has a dreadful speaking voice and is unbelievably ignorant if media reports are to be believed. In more civilised times such people would have been left alone to fail their school exams, get a boring job in the local factory and live a dismal life of poverty on a run-down council estate.

Now, they are encouraged to believe that they could become celebrities – and, of course, they are stupid enough to fall for it.

Despite having absolutely no talent, they are built up by the media, which then take great pleasure in bringing them down again, and all for our perverse amusement. Reality programmes like *Big Brother* may claim to hold a mirror up to society, but they are little more than grotesque freak shows. Goody can't help being a moron any more than Shetty can help being Indian, and yet we are encouraged to hate Goody for her stupidity.

There's something wrong there.

ANC response to Rattray is telling

4 February 2007

President Thabo Mbeki's absurd claim that crime is no big deal in South Africa will do little to comfort the family of David Rattray, who was murdered at his home last weekend.

I first heard of his death while spending a weekend in the Drakensberg Mountains with friends. One from our party received a cellphone call with the distressing news on the Saturday morning and it cast a pall over the whole weekend.

At midday we turned on the SAfm news and there was no mention of the murder. We tuned in again an hour later and there was still no mention of a murder that had taken place the previous evening and which was, by then, common knowledge.

One can only surmise that the minions who run the SABC news desk at the weekend were terrified of upsetting the ANC politburo and the unctuous Commissar Snuki.

I met David Rattray last year when he was invited to speak at a car launch near the Kruger Park. After dinner, we sat in the boma and listened to this magical storyteller relate what had happened at the Battle of Isandlwana on a January day in 1879.

It was a tale told with a mixture of affection, humour and passion which was no mean feat considering how many times Rattray must have told the story before.

When he had finished, he chatted to the assembled motoring hacks and was kind enough to tell me that he enjoyed reading this column every Sunday. It's always an honour when somebody admits to enjoying the Out to Lunch column, but doubly so when it happens to be someone I also admire.

Rattray travelled extensively, telling his wonderful stories and acting as an unpaid brand ambassador for South Africa.

Two close friends from the UK who are regular visitors to South Africa went to listen to him speak in London last October, along with about 500 other people.

They were mesmerised and immediately e-mailed me, suggesting a joint visit to the battlefields in 2008.

I received a short e-mail from them at the weekend expressing their horror and sadness at the news.

That is just one small example of how Rattray enriched so many lives.

One cannot blame Thabo Mbeki for being so blasé about crime. After all, he is a politician and it would never do to admit there's a problem.

Earlier in the year he got perilously close to suggesting that we might have a real crisis, but by the time he was interviewed by Tim Modise, the crisis had been downgraded to a problem. Perhaps somebody pointed out to him that there are now so many criminals within the ANC that his comments could be construed as offensive to many of his colleagues.

Judging by the e-mails I receive, the 'lie and deny' tactics of the ANC are annoying a growing number of people.

The ANC can no longer play the race card because an increasing number of erudite black readers write to tell me how sickened they have become by the party of liberation's greed and cronyism.

Thus far there has been more comment from the ANC about Brett Kebble's death than there has about Rattray's.

That tells you everything you need to know about this government.

FNB debacle is just business as usual

11 February 2007

The real surprise about last week's news that First National Bank had been pressurised into dropping a much-needed anti-crime initiative was the inept and chaotic response from the bank. Obviously such a campaign was going to be controversial, so one wonders why there wasn't a team in place to handle media comment. After all, banks pay an absolute fortune to other key employees, so it would seem sensible to pay top dollar for someone intelligent enough to explain the bank's thinking. Given that many people think such a response from a large corporation is long overdue, it would have been a very easy job.

Instead we were told on radio on Monday that nobody from the bank was available for comment. What should have been a PR triumph for the bank started to look ugly, and eventually FirstRand CEO Paul Harris phoned in to John Robbie's show on Talk Radio 702 to partially explain what was going on.

I am disappointed but not surprised that some business figures were critical of the FNB campaign and wished to distance themselves from it. It has been suggested that they were jealous because they hadn't initiated it themselves and didn't want to be upstaged. A more probable explanation is the prevalence of that modern disease, the fear of not being politically correct. When democracy first arrived back in 1994 we were treated to the hideous spectacle of white businessmen pitching up at official functions in long, flowing Nigerian robes in an attempt to ingratiate themselves with their new political masters. In the boardrooms, the offensive Thomas Baines prints came down to be replaced by township art involving bits of twisted coat hanger and corrugated cardboard. When the Reconstruction and Development Programme was mooted, all sorts of companies came up with money-making schemes vaguely linked to RDP in the hope that this would get them noticed.

White businessmen who had talked about 'k**firs' and how 'they' were getting cheeky at their weekends in the bush with National Party ministers suddenly discovered that black was their favourite colour. It was hilarious to watch.

The relationship between government and business is an odd one. In many instances businessmen are forced to deal with their social and intellectual inferiors. There's nothing a politician loves more than being sucked up to by a rich businessman, particularly a thoroughly dishonest one. We saw that with the late Brett Kebble, the exemplary South African, noble patron of the arts (with other people's money) and benefactor to the previously Porsche-disadvantaged. So business plays the game of sucking up and does whatever it takes to make a profit.

The current Black Economic Empowerment debacle is a case in point. If I were the chairman of an SA company and was told that I didn't have my quota of black management, I would tell the government to get lost. Only when politicians can demonstrate that they have mastered the relatively simple task of spending our taxes and managing a country can they come to me and tell me how to run my business. But that never happens because business has learnt to jump whenever it hears its master's voice. Thanks to FNB, maybe that's about to change.

I'm getting in touch with my inner black

18 February 2007

One wonders why people bother to ask for arms-deal kickbacks (not that they do) when there are such rich pickings to be had from BEE deals.

Who in their right mind would ask for an illegal R21 million when all they really need to do is to put together a deal entitling themselves to a legal, risk-free R475 million shared between four people?

Much comment has been made by Leftie journalists and embittered letter writers about the recent Reunert deal.

All I will say is that I really wish I had been black and disadvantaged, because a R150 million payout would have made it all worthwhile. Personally, I wish Cheryl Carolus well and hope that the money brings her all the happiness she deserves. And Cheryl, ignore those cynics who tell you that money that doesn't really belong to you only brings grief. You just go out and buy yourself some Jimmy Choos. You deserve it.

The best thing about the Reunert deal, though, is that my old friend Wendy Lucas-Bull also got a goody bag with R70 million in it. That's in addition to the goody bags from Lafarge and De Beers.

I've known Wendy for 25 years now, and I have always admired her business focus and her undiminished appetite for money. Meet her at a social occasion and you immediately get the feeling that the conversation will be brief unless you can help her acquire more wealth.

Wendy gives all whiteys hope because she is neither previously disadvantaged nor very black. In fact, when I last saw her she was quite pale. And yet she has managed to crash through the cement ceiling of BEE like Wonder Woman, making us all realise that you don't actually need to be black to be a member of a BEE consortium.

Some psychologists will encourage you to discover your 'inner child' in an attempt to get you to lighten up a bit. In the same vein, I now encourage you to discover your 'inner black' in the hope that, like Wendy, you need never again waste your money on a lottery ticket or contemplate entering a reality game show where the prize money is a paltry R1 million.

I have discovered my inner black and I'm hoping that one of those companies that PIC CEO Brian Molefe is targeting will treat my request for a free handout as sympathetically as Reunert's Boel Pretorius did.

To be honest, with JZ still badgering me for R6 million, I could do with a 'quirk of the structure' deal.

I was wandering around the National Air and Space Museum in Washington a few years ago, stroking the flanks of the Enola Gay and wondering what good use she could be put to just north of the Limpopo, when I stopped in front of the bust of a black man.

He was the first African-American combat pilot and his name was Eugene Bullard; born in 1895, he died in poverty in New York in 1961.

Obviously the Yanks didn't let him fly because he was supposed to be picking cotton in Georgia, so he escaped from racial persecution in the US and flew for the French.

It was only when he made a name for himself with the elite Lafayette Flying Corps that the Yanks wanted to claim him as their own.

'Nuff said, homeboys.

Gentlemen, I await your telephone calls. (Fade column to chorus of 'Ole Man River'.)

ANC politicians not worth it

25 February 2007

I'm trying to get worked up about the ANC's controversial Progressive Business Forum.

According to newspaper reports, the ANC promises to set up a meeting with a Cabinet minister or a senior government official in exchange for money for the ANC's coffers.

It's not clear what is discussed at those meetings but I imagine a few hints are dropped about how difficult it is to get by on a Cabinet minister's salary and how nice it would be to own some free shares in a successful company – or buy a shiny new car at a special price.

So what's all the fuss about then? We know from long and bitter experience that the ANC favours shady businessmen. When Imperial boss Bill Lynch won an international award last year there wasn't a murmur of congratulation from senior politicians in the press (or if there was it was in very small print).

Compare that with the nauseating adulation heaped on the late Brett Kebble.

The ANC won't even discipline dishonest politicians within Parliament and with good reason; if it did there would be very few politicians left. So all those who fiddled their travel expenses keep their jobs and are free to cast about for the next scam knowing that there is no chance they will ever be punished.

Over the past few years the ANC has effectively become the largest organised crime syndicate in the country. Which is why the Mafiosi tactic of calling in money for favours should come as no surprise.

Call it protection money, influence peddling, bribery or just a donation; it all amounts to the same thing. That's the way business is done these days and if you don't like it then emigrate.

I was at a high-profile function recently where the guest speaker was Presidential Rottweiler Essop Pahad.

After he finished speaking, the MC for the evening, Ursula Stapelfeldt, thanked the minister for his 'meaningless' speech which was cause for much mirth around the room.

We tried to work out whether Stapelfeldt had made a mistake but decided she had probably listened carefully to the minister and just said what all of us were already thinking. It was a lot of twaddle and it's frightening to think that such intellectual featherweights are free to roam the planet representing South Africa.

Bearing that in mind, what would you really be getting for your money if you applied for platinum membership of the Progressive Business Forum?

The general feeling among the thinking classes is that there are only about five Cabinet ministers who know what they're doing.

The rest enjoy security of tenure thanks to President Thabo Mbeki's curious policy of refusing to sack the no-hopers. So, for example, you would really need to consider the investment carefully if you wanted to set up a meeting with the health minister.

Even if you enjoy what could be diplomatically termed 'a full and frank discussion', is there any guarantee that the minister concerned will remember who you are when you fax your proposal for a new football stadium through?

Remember that this is primarily a money-making venture and 10 minutes after you left another sucker would have been wheeled in for an exclusive one-on-one.

So I'm afraid I can't get at all worked up about the Progressive Business Forum. It's just further confirmation that the ANC has sold its soul and sunk deeper into the mire of avarice but at least they're no longer being secretive about it.

Lead us from swamp of corruption, Trevor

4 March 2007

Apart from a very brief period early in his reign when he raged about the 'amorphous markets', Finance Minister Trevor Manuel has grown in my estimation over the years.

As the controller of the country's purse strings, he has the most difficult job in government, yet he delivers the goods year after year and manages to keep most people happy – a huge achievement in itself.

When I was younger I used to go to bed fantasising about sex with Bo Derek; these days I go to bed fantasising about Trevor Manuel becoming our next president and leading us out of the fetid swamp of avarice and corruption we seem to have found ourselves in under Mr Mbeki's stewardship.

My fantasies about Bo Derek came to nothing (no pun intended) and I suspect much the same will happen with my nocturnal fantasies about Manuel.

The problem with Manuel as a presidential candidate is that he is a decent man with integrity. When he says he has no business interests, one has no reason to doubt him. All sorts of rumours fly around newsrooms, some with a grain of truth and some purely fantastic, but I have never heard Manuel's name mentioned in connection with anything remotely dodgy. He has devoted his energies to what many of his senior party colleagues should be doing: making the new South Africa a better place for all those who had such high hopes back in 1994.

A quotation of Manuel's caught my attention in last week's *Business Times*. He referred to the scramble for assets across the economy as 'a terrible tragedy'. It's actually worse than that. So great has the problem become that we are likely to destroy all hopes of a peaceful future unless something is done to curb our culture of greed. The only winners are the sleazy influence peddlers and those who have helped themselves from the free-money pot.

Under them lies a seething mass of honest tax-paying citizens whose morals wouldn't allow them to enrich themselves in quirkily structured BEE deals, and, below that seething mass, an even greater seething mass of people are still waiting for houses, jobs, healthcare, education and self-respect. That's a potentially explosive cocktail.

If you read the letters pages of our quality newspapers, you cannot fail to detect a change of mood in the country. There is a growing impatience with a government that is perceived to be soft on crime and so tangled up in its own dirty linen that it daren't even investigate charges against the country's top cop. Business lives in fear of new and even more repressive legislation from a government that has a permanently outstretched hand.

Sophistry is the order of the day and gobbledygook terms like 'fast-tracking' are used without a hint of irony when we all know that what is really meant is the appointment of party loyalists who are incapable of doing the job. Senior government ministers spit venom at people who have had the temerity to leave the country. What was supposed to have become a caring, non-racial society has become just another racially divided African kleptocracy.

At least Manuel realises that the ANC has lost its way, but that's unlikely to bother any of his colleagues who are about to add another R100 million to their ill-gotten personal fortunes. These days it's every man for himself and bugger the consequences. Anyone know of a good guillotine maker?

Affirmative action an insult to black talent

11 March 2007

Last year I delivered at least two after-dinner speeches to professional bodies at which members of the audience walked out in disgust.

It could have been boredom, but my limited research over drinks in the bar afterwards revealed that there had been some racist mutterings followed by a walkout, so let's put it down to disgust.

Obviously I don't go out of my way to alienate members of an audience who have paid to hear me speak, but sometimes these things are unavoidable.

On both occasions the offensive subject matter was affirmative action and the obvious conclusion to be drawn was that those who got up and left must have felt that I was talking about them. Of course, by doing so they drew attention to themselves, which only helped reinforce my point.

The 'offensive' bit was the suggestion that our new social engineering system calls for quotas of previously disadvantaged people to be allowed to qualify as doctors, irrespective of whether they can correctly name parts of the body.

Of course, this shameless fast-tracking doesn't just apply to the medical profession.

It applies to virtually every professional discipline in South Africa, which is presumably why Western Cape Transport and Public Works MEC Marius Fransman warned of a looming skills shortage and suggested a three-year moratorium on affirmative action.

Fortunately, I doubt if I'll still be around when the principle qualification for becoming a doctor is whether or not you walked 20km to school in bare feet, so it's not my problem, it's yours.

Running a society based on the lowest common denominator ultimately produces a nation of losers. An obvious example is team sport. If racial quotas are more important than sporting talent, is it any wonder we throw up so many losing teams?

But exactly the same principle applies to business, and when a government dictates who should be employed and at what level, there are bound to be problems, if only because inadequately qualified people are unfairly expected to do a job for which they have received little or no training.

This wouldn't have been so much of a disaster had a system of mentoring been adopted. Instead, knowledgeable white ooms were forced into early retirement and told their skills were no longer required.

Now, of course, they want them to come out of retirement and sort out all the mix-ups.

In principle there is nothing wrong with the idea of addressing past inequalities, but affirmative action ignores economic realities in favour of vote-winning social tinkering.

Dressing someone up as a doctor and giving them a job in a hospital may be good for their self-esteem, but it won't be long before any shortcomings become obvious.

Pretending that someone has qualified as a civil engineer poses no problem until bridges start collapsing and putting people who know nothing about power stations in charge of the country's electricity supply is fine until the lights keep going out.

The worst thing about affirmative action though is that it devalues genuine black talent because success is assumed to be thanks to the Employment Equity Act.

Whites can gripe about affirmative action, but the people who really should be offended are the many blacks who have made it to the top through hard work, education and talent. They were the ones who didn't walk out during my speeches.

South Africa is worth living for

18 March 2007

This is the column none of you were supposed to read. My gravestone should have read, 'Born 9.12.1952 – Died 7.3.2007' and no doubt would have also carried the words 'RIP. He made his final deadline.'

However, divine providence and some very prompt action from the Parkview police and the superb doctors and nursing staff at Milpark Hospital thwarted the plans of the murderous bastards who broke into my house that evening, and I'm still around to write another day.

The fact that I was bouncing around giving press interviews and making wisecracks the day after I was shot should in no way diminish the physical and mental damage my wife and I suffered that evening. I will no doubt burst into tears for no apparent reason, become vague and withdrawn, feel that life has nothing to offer and exhibit all the usual symptoms of trauma, but since I've been doing all of this for years you won't notice the difference. Anyway, it's nothing that a good Cohiba and a glass of Glenmorangie Madeira Wood Finish can't cure.

What is not going to change is the column. I suggested to the editor that I might take off a week or two because I had been shot. 'Are you dead?' he asked and, just to check, popped into the ICU on the night of the shooting to assess the damage. The doctors told him that, although I had been shot through the left arm, all fingers were in perfect working order. So here I am.

Given the choice of having a catheter inserted or being shot I would opt for being shot any day. Ideally I would choose neither, but you can't run the movie back and press delete so the bullet that is lodged in my pelvis is a reality, as is the swollen and bruised abdomen and the bloody arm.

Normally this would be an ideal recipe for gloom and self-pity, but I am determined to regard this whole dreadful business in a positive light. I will definitely not be leaving South Africa and my optimism for the future of this country has been strengthened rather than weakened. We live in the most beautiful country and are blessed with the finest people you could imagine, therefore good must eventually triumph over evil. If I can believe that, then so can you and you must – otherwise we are all lost. Warfare is all about breaking down the spirit of the people and our rampant crime is a particularly ugly form of warfare.

The word 'tsunami' is loosely bandied about these days but it's the only word I can think of to describe the reaction to my shooting. The energy I have gained from the hundreds of supportive letters, SMSs, e-mails and cards I have received has been quite phenomenal (they will all be read) and I am feeling, if not looking, 100%. This incident must be used positively and it is my intention to become far more involved with my local community-policing forum and with the fight against crime in general.

In the few lines left I'd like to thank fellow members of the media for their tremendous support, the police and medics who looked after this pathetic bleeding figure on the night of 7 March, the doctors and staff at Milpark Hospital and particularly you, the wonderful readers of the *Sunday Times*, who bought tears of gratitude to my eyes. Bless you and thank you.

An equal-opportunity lethal barb
for 13 years

25 March 2007

This week the Out to Lunch column celebrates its 13th birthday, making it the longest-running column of that name ever to have appeared in the Careers section of the *Sunday Times* in our proud 101-year history.

This is a remarkable achievement in itself, but even more so for someone who isn't even a trained journalist. It vindicates all those who claim that bullshit baffles brains.

While one of my fellow columnists has his very own page in the main section of the newspaper (which he can't even fill and sublets to advertisers) I remain banished to the Bantustan of the *Sunday Times*, miles away from the real news and comment and with no running water or electricity. This obvious slight would offend thinner-skinned men, but I realise that we middle-aged white boys are damn lucky to have jobs. A shack in the Careers section is better than no shack at all.

Over the years the column has sought to be, in the words of my editor, 'an equal-opportunity dispenser of lethal barbs' and my weekly hate mail suggests that I'm succeeding admirably. Unfortunately, the volume of hostile mail I now receive means that I can only skim some of the more verbose offerings; some I don't bother to read at all if I can think of something better to do (which I usually can).

However, I realise it must be therapeutic for many of you to write these letters and they do occasionally give me a good laugh, so please don't stop. To those of you who have followed the column over the past 13 years and regularly send e-mails and letters of encouragement, I can only apologise for not being able to reply individually to all of you.

However, know that they are greatly appreciated.

One of the key ingredients for the success of a column like Out to Lunch is press freedom. I know I regularly attack what I perceive to be the failings of the government, but without a free press I would never be able to do that. I am aware that much of what I write personally offends those in power, and I make no apology for that. We clearly have ideological differences and there's nothing wrong with some healthy public debate. Who's to say I'm right anyway? Maybe the correct way to run a new democracy really is to enrich key political figures beyond the dreams of avarice and cultivate connections with influential gangsters.

The point is that, ideological differences aside, I am free to write these things and for that we must all be grateful to the ANC. Once we lose the right to fair public criticism, we are on the slippery slope to Zanufication.

When the column first began in March 1994, I reckoned on sticking with it for three years, maximum, and then looking for a real job. Thirteen years later and I'm still looking for a real job, but there doesn't seem to be a huge demand in the corporate world for opinionated loudmouths.

So the plan is to carry on knocking out the required number of words every week in an attempt to either make or ruin your Sunday morning for at least another two years. Then, when XXX (Sorry ... can't tell you his name yet. I haven't finalised the election campaign.) has become the new president, I'm off to London as the new SA ambassador. At least, that's what he's promised me in return for my considerable influence. Oh, the joys of belonging to the powerful fourth estate!

JZ stopped by ICU to play some Scrabble

1 April 2007

Lying on my back in the Milpark Hospital ICU a few weeks ago gave me a leisurely few hours to stare at the roof tiles and think about life.

To be absolutely honest, there's not much else you can do in ICU. You're wired up like a surround-sound home theatre. You've got a catheter inserted, a blood-pressure sleeve on your arm, a thermometer cord in your groin and a needle stuck in your vein with a saline drip permanently attached plus an extra inlet for the drugs they pump into you throughout the night.

Even if you want to wander over to the window for a bit of fresh air you can't because you're a prisoner in your own hospital bed.

Just to make sure you don't go walkabout while wired, they have bars on the side of the bed to prevent you escaping. That means the fresh fruit you've been sent by well-wishers sits on a table just out of range. I spent at least 30 frustrating minutes doing a passable impersonation of an orang-utan, reaching in vain through the bars for a fresh peach.

Just as I was dozing off to the melodic bleeping of the life-support monitors, Jacob Zuma came through the door surrounded by an army of press photographers. I felt a bit bad because I'd already asked the nurses to tell Thabo Mbeki I was too tired to see him.

I think that's probably what led to his petulant outburst on the ANC website, the one about white boys getting themselves shot by intruders in the privacy of their own homes and then blabbing about it to all their mates in the press.

This sort of selfish, racist behaviour is the type of thing that's likely to lose us the 2010 World Cup, and if that happens then a whole bunch of connected cronies won't make nearly as much money.

Anyway, Jacob pulled up a chair, beamed at me and helped himself to a ripe mango from the fruit basket before peeling me a peach, cutting it into slices and feeding them to me one by one. The press flash guns popped and a cynical thought flashed through my mind. Maybe JZ was only there for the photo opportunity. Then another thought occurred to me. If JZ is already here, can Winnie be far behind?

Dismissing any impure thoughts of political opportunism, I asked JZ to sing me the refrain from his now famous 'bring me my machine gun' ditty. He immediately started swaying and singing that lovely melody with his mellifluous voice.

Gradually the entire ICU ward joined in, apart from the guy in the corner who'd been involved in a car accident and had his jaw wired. We all hugged and cried afterwards and JZ explained that it's nothing personal, it's just a song.

Then we started to play Scrabble. One of JZ's many bodyguards had bought along a personalised Scrabble set with 11 Xs, 12 Zs and 9 Qs. The board looked much like the familiar Scrabble board except for the fact that the triple-word score tiles were missing.

I queried this and JZ laughed and showed me a page of adhesive red triple-word stickers. 'Whenever you have a high-scoring word, you just stick your own triple-score sticker on whatever tile takes your fancy,' he explained with a mischievous chuckle.

Just as I was about to put down my first word, the effects of the morphine wore off and I realised that, like the new South Africa, it had all been a strange and terrifying hallucination.

Pre-recorded birdsong for Fort Bullard now

8 April 2007

I have been taken to task by a few readers over my optimism for this country after my shooting four weeks ago. They suggest, in the kindest possible way, that I should remove my head from the sand and get out while I still can.

They may well be right. Over the past few weeks I have also had cause to question my optimism, particularly after I received a signed death threat from a student at the University of KwaZulu-Natal. He expressed joy at the fact I had survived the shooting because it would give him the opportunity to finish the job – and he wouldn't miss.

The journey from the back door to the compost heap is fraught with danger, so I now wear my panic button whenever I carry the potato peelings out. Similarly, emptying of the rubbish bins into the dustbin and the weekly transportation of the dustbin to the street for collection has become an exercise planned with military precision.

My young nephew in Scotland was to be the latest family member to visit, in July. I was to spend two weeks showing him this beautiful country and introducing him to some of the wonderful people who live here. That is no longer going to happen. I told my brother that I didn't feel we could guarantee his son's safety if he visited South Africa, not only in our home but on something as mundane as a shopping trip to the local mall.

Can you imagine being custodian of a 14-year-old boy and having to phone his father to say he was stabbed to death or shot by intruders who wanted his cellphone?

My brother was greatly relieved. He hadn't wanted to offend me by saying he was unhappy about his son's proposed visit, and was pleased that I had taken the initiative to suggest that it be cancelled. I have also told two other sets of friends who were planning to visit this year that we are unable to host them unless they sign legal documents absolving us from all liability should they be attacked in our home.

I'll send them an SA Tourism DVD as compensation.

My house is now surrounded by spikes on the walls; laser beams guard the outside access areas, a security camera watches the gate, there are bars on the bedroom windows and ugly steel security gates on the doors.

On a warm summer's evening we now sit indoors with all the doors and windows closed, the security system on – and use an electric fan to keep cool.

In our innocence we used to sit in our garden enjoying a glass of wine, listening to birdsong and watching barbets and weavers build their nests.

That's obviously asking for trouble, so one evening I put on a bullet-proof jacket and ventured out to the garden to film the sunset and the birds. Now we sit indoors watching a recording of our garden and the birds on TV. It's so much safer.

The idea of inviting friends around for a braai is quite preposterous, and going for a late-night swim completely out of the question. In fact, going for a swim at any time of day is risky, and I'm looking around for a waterproof panic button.

It's an appalling way to live, but it hasn't dampened my enthusiasm or optimism for the future of this country a bit. The sad thing is that our equality has been achieved in such a perverse way. Now we are all afraid and none of us is truly free.

Crime is an excellent business proposition

15 April 2007

Crime, like any business venture, essentially comes down to an assessment of the risk–reward ratio. Simply put, if the potential reward is substantially higher than the risk then you have a good business.

Absurd as it may seem, the law in this country favours the criminal over the victim of crime.

So, for example, you are not permitted to shoot a gun-wielding thug who has broken into your home with the intention of robbing you and raping the female members of your family. And if he so much as grazes his hands on the security spikes you put on the top of the wall, he has a legal case against you.

If you shoot him he will be airlifted, at the taxpayer's expense, to a well-equipped private hospital and given the finest medical care your money can buy. The government's perverse view is that we don't want to be accused by the international community of offering our violent criminals anything but the best when it comes to healthcare, even if we do have to handcuff them to the bed.

If he shoots you, then you'll first need to prove that you are a member of a reliable medical aid scheme before anything can happen. Failing that, you will have to join the queue at a public hospital. The average bill for a gunshot wound is around R40 000, but if you need extensive surgery that amount can easily escalate to over R100 000.

Even if your medical aid coughs up, you'll still find yourself chipping in a hefty amount for the bits not covered by medical aid.

If you're unfortunate enough not to be adequately covered, a gunshot wound could easily bankrupt you. No such worries for the state-sponsored criminal, though.

I have been hugely impressed at the dedication shown by the police officers involved in the investigation of my recent shooting. I can't help thinking that if more of us got involved with our local police or even visited the police station to thank them for risking their lives for us and offering some words of encouragement then we would have a far more motivated police force.

However, it soon became apparent that, despite their best efforts, the police are woefully under-resourced and over–stretched.

Consequently, the chance of an arrest and a successful prosecution are slim. That substantially lowers the risk side of the equation and makes crime an attractive and glamorous occupation, even for those who could make an honest living if they really wanted to.

The culture of greed cultivated by the government must be held partly to blame for the current crime wave. Ostentatious displays of wealth are encouraged because they supposedly demonstrate that one person is 'better' than another because he or she has a faster car, a more modern cellphone, more expensive shoes, a flashier watch, and so on. Some people suggest that such crass vulgarity is good for the poor because it gives them hope.

Who can blame people with no education and low self-esteem for believing that a pair of trainers or a designer-label golf shirt will earn them the respect they so desperately crave?

What we urgently need is a strong leader to unite the nation against the common enemy of crime. Instead, we have a man who has so little confidence in the future of this country that he is building a wall to protect himself.

Offer Zimbabweans dignity – and visas

22 April 2007

It's hard to imagine what life must be like in Zimbabwe for the average citizen but miserable would be a pretty good guess.

We know that Mad Bob's goons regularly beat up his political opponents and abduct, torture and murder any journalists critical of his repulsive regime.

The terror campaign which had initially been confined to the capital has now apparently spread countrywide and Mugabe has formed a special paramilitary unit to crack as many Zimbabwean skulls as possible.

Reports suggest that more than 600 people have been beaten and tortured in detention and my guess is that figure is bound to rise.

If you keep your nose clean in Zimbabwe and wave the Zanu-PF flag whenever Mad Bob's motor cavalcade passes you have little to worry about. Admittedly you will starve to death and what money you have will be worth considerably less tomorrow morning, but at least you might avoid a good hiding by the police.

Hardly surprising then that so many Zimbabweans have decided to jump the razor-wire and head for South Africa, land of the free.

I was at a lunch the other day and someone who should know reckoned there could be as many as 5 million illegal Zimbabweans in this country. Even if the true figure is half that, it still represents a sizeable percentage of the SA population.

Various newspaper articles have described how highly qualified Zimbabweans are having to eke out a living as security guards or waiters. Desperate as they are, they run the risk of being exploited because they are not legal citizens and there's no chance of them filing an official complaint.

Mad Bad Bob has destroyed their country and they have no identity in this country and, therefore, no chance of building a legitimate new life.

Our government's stand on Zimbabwe is an international disgrace, particularly for a party that fought for racial equality and justice. 'Quiet diplomacy' is one of those meaningless phrases that politicians like to bandy about to persuade the rest of us that they are aware of the problem. Loosely translated it means 'we can't be bothered to do anything and, besides, we're hoping the problem just goes away'. Well it hasn't and, thanks to the ANC government's spinelessness, things are bound to get worse.

We are morally obliged to do something positive for our neighbours from the north. If the Zimbabwean refugees, who have left their loved ones behind, braved the razor-wire and made it to South Africa, are not welcomed and absorbed into South African society, then we store up unimaginable problems for ourselves in the future.

The ANC has never once received one of my helpful suggestions in the spirit in which it has been intended. So let me try again.

If we like to think of ourselves as a civilised society then we must offer Zimbabweans hope for the future. We urgently need skills in this country and Zimbabweans bring with them many of those and not necessarily at the expense of local jobs.

So please, Mr Mbeki, stop being a pipe-smoking intellectual for once and set up a fast-tracking system to legalise these unfortunate people. Having betrayed them for so long, it's the least we can do.

Flaunting wealth no fun unless to the poor

29 April 2007

What would be the point of being ostentatious if there was nobody to impress?

I ask this question because the debate is hotting up on whether or not it's good manners to rub the noses of the poor in the dirt by driving slowly past them in your new R1-million limo.

The 'new' South African thinking is that it's perfectly acceptable to flaunt your material possessions, even if you are up to your neck in credit card debt. The problem is who to flaunt them to.

If you hang out at the sort of fashionable gatherings attended by my colleagues Gwen Gill and Craig Jacobs then the chances are that you're mixing with people from a similar background. Apart from the odd journo, nobody is likely to be impressed with your R250 000 Speake-Marin wristwatch. People who dress outrageously at these do's are regarded simply as outrageously dressed people. Nobody gives a fig what the outfit cost because if it's simply a matter of laying down the cash, then lead me to the designer.

Sipping expensive malt whisky, puffing on a cigar that costs as much as 200 cigarettes and stuffing yourself with oysters flown in from France may annoy people like Max du Preez but it's what you're supposed to do at these thrashes; particularly if someone else is paying. So, as an exercise in conspicuous consumption, social occasions are pretty useless.

Much of the satisfaction of luxury-item ownership is derived from the knowledge that what you own is unaffordable to most people. Another is that the thing that cost so much is not essential. That partly explains why certain handbags, jewel-encrusted cellphones and even women's shoes sell for amounts of money that could feed a family of four for a year. And that's the whole point: the social injustice of one person being able to spend so much on an overpriced and completely unnecessary item while fellow human beings barely have enough to eat.

Years ago I went to a function in Maputo. It was the opening of the first Checkers store there and various dignitaries and hacks were invited to celebrate, drink huge quantities and eat as much as they liked.

A tall wire fence had been erected around the newly constructed car park to keep out the riff-raff. That night, as we feasted, hundreds of hungry faces were pressed up against the wire, watching in disbelief as we gorged on food we didn't really need. This was real conspicuous consumption, and you could feel the envy and hatred coming through the fence.

That's the problem with the poor. Like pit bull terriers, they are unreliable. One minute they're licking your face and telling you what a nice car you drive, and the next they have a knife at your throat and want the car keys and the contents of your wallet.

Personally I think you're asking for trouble by flaunting your wealth in a country like South Africa where the have-nots far outnumber the haves. However, that's a matter of good judgment and taste, and who am I to snigger at such crass vulgarity?

What does worry me, though, is the suggestion that many of those who flaunt their wealth do so only because they have very little else worth flaunting.

Name and shame offensive bloggers

6 May 2007

If imitation is the sincerest form of flattery then Fred Khumalo and I should feel very flattered indeed. Every day there are 120 000 new blog sites registered – a staggering 43 million a year. According to blog search engine Technorati, there are already 70 million blog sites registered worldwide. Admittedly the majority of the bloggers get bored rather quickly and don't bother to update their sites, but that's still 70 million people (higher than the population of the UK) who desperately want to be columnists.

It's comforting to know that, should Fred or I decide to take a sabbatical, there's no shortage of people available to hold the fort. The only snag is the quality, or lack of it.

Allow me to explain what I mean. I used to play air guitar with a band called Deep Purple. My playing was perfect, I had attitude and I even smashed my air guitar at the end of the number. The reason I played air guitar is that I couldn't play real guitar very well so I was forced to dwell in this fantasy world where my guitar playing meant something only to me. I should point out that this was years ago when I was still young and foolish. These days I play air tenor saxophone, which is far more challenging.

Most blog sites are the air guitars of journalism. They're cobbled together by people who wouldn't stand a hope in hell of getting a job in journalism, mainly because they have very little to say. It's rather sad how many people think the tedious minutiae of their lives will be of any interest to anyone else.

It's even sadder when someone reads them.

Many bloggers prefer to remain anonymous and with good reason. The content of their sites is so moronic that even their best friends would disown them if they knew they were the authors. As with most things in life, something that costs nothing is usually worth nothing and that puzzles me. Are there really 70 million bloggers out there hoping that their writing talents will be recognised, or is this just another example of modern narcissism?

Unlike the world of newsprint, there are no rules out there in the blogosphere and that makes it a very confusing place for the consumer. I have no objection to reading my *Sunday Times* on the Internet because I know the content has been through the same process as the print edition. I do, however, object to some anonymous, scrofulous nerd pumping meaningless drivel into cyberspace at all hours of the day and night simply because he can't find a girl to sleep with him. These are the sort of wackos who gun down their fellow students at university. I visited a site the other day that was so hideously racist that it would have qualified its publisher for a long spell in prison if it had appeared in print. So what's the difference? How come newspapers and magazines have to carry the names of their editors and publishers and watch their content and websites don't? I'm told that it's possible to track down the author of any offensive website and perhaps that's what the government should be doing instead of looking at legislation to gag legitimate publications. Better still, maybe it's time the print journalists named and shamed some of the more offensive anonymous bloggers and published their physical addresses. Then I can start a blog site called printrevenge.com and bore you all with the details.

In the blogosphere everybody's a scream

13 May 2007

I'm feeling rather like Moses must have felt after he parted the Red Sea ... a bit smug at my own extreme cleverness and a little surprised that it worked.

I knew when I wrote it that last week's column on bloggers was bound to draw a few comments.

What I didn't realise was quite how many. I'm told by excited colleagues that I single-handedly caused the largest amount of daily traffic ever on the South African blogosphere.

If you visit one of the local web aggregators you will find a box with my name writ large (or you would have last week) indicating that I am now the prime topic of conversation within the murky world of the blogosphere. Let's pause to savour this achievement for a moment.

A 50-something freelance columnist in the print media can attract far more attention from one article than the much younger bloggers have ever achieved. That's game set and match to the print media in my book.

What was of particular interest (once someone showed me how to access them) was the quality of many of the comments.

What a bunch of humourless bed-wetters some of these bloggers are. Check for yourselves if you don't believe me. Go to the *Sunday Times* website and read some of the comments just to get the general flavour. Don't waste too much time on them because you've probably got much better things to do. Some of these people are clearly platinum-club members of life's losers' lounge. If they swam with dolphins they would probably get savaged.

One early commentator (who I believe is an ordained priest in the Church of the Latter-day Blog) unimaginatively dubbed the whole affair Bullardgate and claims I owe South African bloggers an apology. He went on at great length to froth and splutter (don't these guys have jobs?) detailing my manifold sins and wickedness and, just for good measure, suggested that the *Sunday Times* was also at fault for publishing it.

This is quite interesting and was a recurring theme among many bloggers. Apparently freedom of speech is not as deeply cherished in the blogosphere as it is in the print media.

Apart from a lack of humour and incredible sensitivity, it seems that many bloggers' natural response is to lash out, rather like cornered badgers. I was hoping for a general exchange of moderately insulting banter, but I have to say that the majority of the comments fall way short when it comes to intelligent invective. Most is little more than playground name calling, which is very boring. On the other hand, I suppose if you're dumb enough to take such a deliberately inflammatory article seriously then you're also too stupid to phrase an elegant riposte.

However, my new criticism of bloggers is this: not only can most of them not write, some of them can't even read.

The response to last week's article bore little relevance to the actual wording. Unless those who complained really are the anonymous, scrofulous nerds I spoke of then they surely have nothing to fear.

The final irony is that, thanks to the bloggers, I now have my own blog, which serves me right. I should have kept my mouth shut.

Why pretend the poor will inherit anything?

20 May 2007

I was rapped across the knuckles recently for unflattering comments I made about the poor.

Predictably, the complaints didn't come from the poor themselves but from their conscious-ridden middle-class representatives.

So this week I thought I would examine our collective hypocrisy when it comes to the poor.

Let's be brutally honest. None of us really likes the poor. We may pretend to be concerned about them because it makes us seem like nice people, but how often do you see pictures of leading business figures and politicians hanging out with the poor?

Not often. Only when an election looms will you see politicians shedding crocodile tears and arranging photo opportunities with a family of toxic-waste dump scavengers.

For the rest of the time the poor are ignored, and with good reason; they are very boring. They don't throw great parties, they can't get you a low-price 4x4, they can't cut you in on a lucrative arms deal and they can't introduce you to glamorous people from the world of television.

In fact, apart from making the rest of us feel so good about having money, the poor really don't have any redeeming features.

Our smartly dressed politicians far prefer attending a swanky party with a fully stocked bar than picking their way through puddles of raw sewage on the banks of the Jukskei River, and who can blame them?

When it comes to cars there are few politicians who can resist the temptation to drive the sort of wildly expensive vehicle that makes their comments on the plight of the poor sound rather hollow. After all, it's the taxpayer that settles the bill and there's no reason for politicians to travel around in expensive German limos when a perfectly good Toyota or Nissan would do the job just as well.

If I were a politician I would probably behave in the same way, the only exception being that I would have been elected on a non poor-vote ticket. I wouldn't feign interest in a lost cause. The poor may always be with us but they will also always be economically unviable and that means they will always be whiners.

When politicians talk about the need to uplift the poor they haven't a clue what they're saying.

What is this upliftment anyway? Is it a better class of poverty being offered, or do politicians really believe they can create opportunities that will lift the poor from their abject, wretched lives and bring them lasting happiness?

If so, we've been waiting nearly 14 years for this miracle and nothing much has happened.

Wouldn't it be much kinder to stop pretending and just tell the poor that, with the exception of water delivery and electricity they can't afford, there's not much the government can do for them?

That way nobody would be kidding anyone else and the poor would just have to get used to the idea that they probably did something bad in a previous life. The moneyed classes could live a guilt-free existence and the poor could do what they do best ... form the backdrop for foreign television documentaries about South Africa's readiness to host the 2010 World Cup.

ANC succession as important as 1994

27 May 2007

The most extraordinary thing about the ANC's leadership succession is that, after almost 14 years in power, nobody in the party has been groomed to take South Africa into the future.

It's hardly surprising in the circumstances that the ruling party plays down the importance of the leadership race and pretends it's of no consequence, other than to those within the higher echelons of the ANC church.

It is, of course, the most important political event since the 1994 election, and the result will determine this country's future position (or lack thereof) on the world stage.

If the country is led by a buffoon of the stature of Idi Amin then all we can look forward to is Hollywood making a movie in about 20 years' time about our demise.

I also find interesting the official reaction whenever someone so much as suggests that he or she would be available as a potential candidate for the presidency of the ANC and, by implication, of the country. These things are not supposed to be discussed outside the four walls of the power brokers' offices apparently, which rather makes a mockery of the idea that South Africa is a democracy.

Tokyo Sexwale's availability was revealed on the BBC programme *Hard Talk* and that seems to have upset a few people. How dare Sexwale answer a direct question from one of our former colonial oppressors without clearing it first with the politburo?

The fact that Sexwale is personable and a successful businessman also apparently counts against him – if we are to believe anything the ANC Youth League has to say on the matter. The leadership of the Youth League doesn't like the fact that Sexwale has been financially successful and, if I understand them correctly, they don't think it would be a good idea if the country were to be run along business lines because that might mean some cost cutting and a concentration on return on investment. Obviously that wouldn't be good for the League which enjoys the reputation of being a degenerate bunch of freeloaders.

Perhaps it's time SA was run as if it were a business. Cabinet ministers would no longer enjoy security of tenure for life but would be held accountable for their mistakes. If the country experienced lengthy power cuts then there would be no magnificent year-end bonuses. Instead, somebody's head would be on the block.

I can't think of a successful business that doesn't have a succession plan for key executives. This is partly because corporates are under constant scrutiny from analysts, who invariably think they know how to run the business better than the CEO.

On a more serious note though, it makes good business sense to have a continuity plan and this is why the ANC is such a confused bunch of ditherers. Why else would they be so sensitive whenever the media mention the subject?

Unless fortune smiles and the moment presents the man, South Africa as we know it today could implode in December. The bad news is that there's absolutely nothing we can do about it. The good news is that the new president will be presenting the World Cup to England in 2010.

Ditch friends who don't live in the right areas

3 June 2007

I was thrilled to read in the *Financial Mail* recently that I live in what is known as a 'golden corridor' suburb.

According to the article, 'all SA major cities now have golden corridors of super prime suburbs that would be the first choice of most home buyers if they could afford it'.

Apparently I live in one of the most desirable suburbs with access to the best domestic infrastructure and I can take even more comfort from the knowledge that, when property prices rise, they will rise fastest in the golden corridor suburbs and that my house has a better chance than most of retaining its value when the market slumps. So there.

But if you don't live in a golden corridor, don't despair. There are also the up-and-coming silver corridor suburbs, where the property prices are also expected to perform well. Unfortunately they'll probably never become golden corridor suburbs because that would mean the golden corridor suburbs would have to upgrade and become platinum corridor.

What lies beyond the silver corridor suburbs is vague but it's obviously not very desirable so I'll just call it housing.

Where you live, rather like what car you drive, is designed to let other people know where you think you fit on the social scale. When I lived in London I started out by renting a flat in a place called Raynes Park. It had an SW19 area code, which wasn't bad, but it wasn't as fashionable as Wimbledon's SW20 area code so I didn't get invited to many parties.

The higher you went up the SW codes the better the area became so I moved into a flat with three girls in trendy Chelsea just off the Kings Road in the SW3 area and suddenly my social life blossomed. The girls all had very rich daddies with massive houses in the country and the mantelpiece in the sitting room was permanently covered in gold-embossed invitations to parties.

Unfortunately the lease ran out so we had to go our separate ways. I decided that I couldn't move down from SW3 so there was only one way to go and that was up. I moved into a flat, this time with just two girls, in SW1 right next to Westminster Cathedral and conveniently close to the Army and Navy store, which, in those days, had a mini food hall to rival Harrods. But I had university friends who had rather unwisely chosen to save on rent and use the money for drink. Some lived in Putney, which was always sneeringly referred to as 'south of the river' and one of them actually chose to live in a hideously unfashionable SE area. They led miserable, cloistered lives.

Our golden and silver corridors and the unmentionable bits beyond are the South African equivalent of any major city's desirable and undesirable areas. For example, in New York, Upper East Side Manhattan has always been more fashionable than the Upper West Side where John Lennon was shot.

All this gives us a wonderful opportunity to ditch racism once and for all and, instead, to become corridor snobs. From now on when I read the letters pages in the newspapers I will check the writer's address and if it isn't golden corridor I will ignore the letter. I am also going through my address book and plan to terminate any friendships with people living outside the golden and silver corridors. It's tough, I know, but sometimes you have to be cruel to be kind.

Nobody asks Mbeki the burning question

10 June 2007

CNBC Africa was launched on 1 June with a one-hour interview with President Thabo Mbeki.

I was supposed to have been at the launch party but had to make my apologies at the last moment due to a family emergency. I did, however, turn on my television and watch the first broadcast.

The idea was that President Mbeki would field questions from around the world and would also answer questions from the invited audience. The local questioners coincidentally also happened to represent the four sponsors, so one got the distinct impression that the programme content had been choreographed to avoid any embarrassment to host or guest.

The foreign questioners, beamed in via a gigantic screen in the studio, were less tame but seemed bewildered by the President's rambling replies. I really tried to pay attention, but I have to say that Thabo Mbeki is a master of obfuscation. Maybe I became mesmerised by the constant movement of his hands to the extent that I entirely missed the point of what he was trying to say.

When the President had finished speaking, the presenter would ask the bewildered questioner on the big screen whether his or her question had been answered satisfactorily. Judging by the expressions on their faces I would have said the answer was no, but no one was inconsiderate enough to upset the precision timing of the one-hour show by saying so.

Nobody asked the one question one would have expected to hear on a new business channel. Unhappily, the launch of CNBC Africa coincided with the largest national strike in the history of South Africa. As is well known, the government is offering a 6% increase and the unions are demanding 12%. I should have thought one of the questions on CNBC Africa's maiden broadcast should have been along the lines of: 'Mr President, you've just awarded yourselves healthy increases, way above the inflation rate, as MPs, and yet you expect the people who work for SA Inc. to be happy with 6%. You and your colleagues have frequently criticised the gap between management and workers' salaries in the private sector, so how do you justify the wide gap in the public sector?'

That would have made a more memorable first broadcast.

I find myself unusually sympathetic to the demands of the public servants, until I hear about them going on a rampage and destroying property or invading hospitals.

There were also reports of hospital staff being harassed if they turned up to work. That is precisely the type of loutish behaviour that loses public sympathy and demonstrates that the union officials have little control over the more unruly elements within their ranks. It might even suggest that the officials approve of a bit of mayhem.

This is a pity because most people I have spoken to feel the cause of a greater increase than 6% is just. There have been the obvious comments about nobody noticing the difference between civil servants being on strike and being at work but we all know that without them the country really would grind to a halt.

What the unions need to do is to control the hooligan element, which would win wider public sympathy for their demands. A 6% increase on an already low salary is an insult and most public servants deserve more.

Zuma should preserve his dignity and retire

17 June 2007

Considering Jacob Zuma's rather jaundiced view of the media, I thought it was sporting of the World Editors Forum to invite him to address them over lunch during their recent conference in Cape Town.

They were probably wise not to opt for an after-dinner speech because JZ can go on a bit and it's quite likely he would have started swaying rhythmically and singing about wanting his machine gun.

In a rather chilling hint of things to come under a Zuma presidency, he effectively told the editors that the media threatened their own freedom by asking too many difficult questions. Zuma thinks the media have given him a rough ride and to teach them the real meaning of democracy and freedom he is suing some of them (this columnist included).

The chairman of the South African Press Council asked Zuma why he hadn't complained to the press Ombudsman if he felt he had been wronged, a route that would have been way cheaper than legal recourse. Zuma replied that this would have led simply to an apology and 'that would be the end of the story'.

So what exactly does Zuma want? He has gone on record as saying that suing poor journalists for absurdly large amounts in damages is not about the money. And yet he has now admitted that he isn't interested in an apology. Which can only mean that the abuse of the legal process is all part of his presidential campaign circus and should be taken no more seriously than Zuma suddenly having become a priest a few weeks ago. Within the next few months I fully expect him to embrace Islam, become a kwaito singer and start breeding prize orchids in an attempt to win over more of the electorate.

I wouldn't go so as far as suggesting that if Jacob Zuma didn't exist it would be necessary to invent him, but his amiable-buffoon persona makes him a very welcome addition to the political scenery. He's rarely out of the news (or the courts for that matter) and I have yet to see a photograph of him not beaming happily. The dark, litigious clouds constantly hanging over his head would have destroyed lesser men but JZ just shrugs off his many troubles and gets on with life. This is an admirable quality in anyone – except a presidential hopeful.

Zuma's criticism of the media is that they went beyond their bounds when reporting on his rape trial and on the possibility that he might have had his hand perilously close to, if not actually in, the arms deal cookie jar. I can sympathise with JZ on this but when you hold yourself up as a symbol of family values and head the country's moral regeneration programme you can't really blame the cartoonists, columnists and commentators for lampooning you when you are literally caught with your pants down. We do have a constitutional right to free speech, after all, and ridiculing errant politicians has been a favourite occupation of the press for centuries.

Think how ridiculous it would be if George Dubya sued every cartoonist, TV show and journalist he believed offended his dignity.

The solution is simple. Slip out of the public eye for good and you become entitled to far greater privacy because you're no longer newsworthy. Retirement in KwaZulu-Natal must be an attractive option for a man with so much dignity to protect.

You don't write, you don't call ...

24 June 2007

D ue to an unusually hectic travel schedule, I have had to write the *Out to Lunch* column several weeks in advance.

This poses various problems, not the least of which is topicality. I haven't a clue what you'll be talking about in two or three weeks' time, although I'm willing to bet that strikes, power cuts, Paris Hilton and the ANC succession battle won't be too far from the headlines. Worse, though, is the possibility that something really devastating will happen and my column will completely ignore it. Which is precisely why I have gone to all the trouble of telling you that this particular column was written over two weeks ago.

Should Table Mountain have become a volcano and spewed molten lava and hot ash all over the Mother City, then I apologise in advance for not mentioning it in greater detail this week.

The other problem with a long absence from one's desk is that the e-mails mount up, and when I get back I am faced with about 600 of them to read. Yes, I know you can get expensive hand-held gadgets which are part cellphone and part office-on-the-move and you can pick up your e-mails on them. I had lunch with a friend recently, and he had one which he kept looking at to check his latest e-mails. He asked if I had one and I told him that I couldn't think of anything more horrendous.

A cellphone is bad enough because once you own one you are expected to leave it on and be available at all hours. I commit the unforgivable sin of turning mine off and not answering calls that don't display a number.

I also don't have a voicemail box, partly because I haven't a clue how to set it up, but mainly because I don't want to spend my money listening to long messages from people I don't know telling me what to write in this column next week. If you've got such great ideas, get a column of your own.

The idea of something constantly bleeping to tell me I have a new e-mail fills me with dread. These things seem like great gadgets to have, but the reality is that they are energy-sapping because you feel compelled to leave them on. That means you can never again enjoy privacy. In the good old days of normal telephony, you could choose to ignore a ringing phone.

That suggested to the caller that you were out and there were no recriminations. Then came the dreaded answerphone, which brought with it the responsibility to return the call – and that's when the whole communication rot set in.

The cellphone ring can be ignored if you have a strong enough will, but callers find it far more irritating than ignoring a land line because you are supposed to carry your cellphone wherever you go. That means you are expected to answer it, irrespective of whether it's convenient or not.

I've found a simple Luddite solution for the e-mailers. I've left an out-of-office reply telling them that I am away and will probably return to a few hundred unread e-mails. Since that will induce a panic attack in me, I propose to delete the whole lot unread on the basis that life is simply too short to wade through them all. In fact, I might make this a permanent solution to a growing problem and save myself several hours each working day by deleting all my incoming e-mails, unread. It doesn't do to be too accessible.

Somebody get those breakers to shut up

1 July 2007

The only problem with the sea is that it doesn't have a volume control.

A few weeks ago I spent five nights in what I thought would be an idyllic cottage at Storms River National Park.

The cottage is as near to the sea as it could possibly be and all day and night the waves pound the rocks and send plumes of spray into the air. A particularly heavy swell sends a tremor through the rocks that rattles the crockery in the kitchen.

The windows of the cottage I stayed in slide wide open, making it possible to sit comfortably indoors while the elements do their thing outside. This, for a city dweller, ought to be holiday heaven but it isn't.

Apart from the occasional house alarm going off and nocturnal gunshots, my particular part of the golden corridor is very quiet in Joburg at night.

Wake at three in the morning and all is silent. It's so quiet that if a neighbour three blocks away has a party I can hear the music and feel the tremors of the bass.

So quite what possessed me to book a holiday in a cottage by the sea, I don't know. It must be something to do with imagining that the grass is greener on the other side.

Not that I'm complaining. The people at South African National Parks do an astoundingly good job. The staff are friendly and helpful, booking is a doddle, the prices are right, the accommodation is clean and well equipped and the beds are comfortable.

The camp at Storms River occupies some of the most beautiful real estate in the world and I challenge you to find a substantially better view than the one from the restaurant.

So, all things considered, it should be a wonderful place to go to relax and enjoy the splendour of the South African scenery. Except, that is, for the sea.

The first night was fine because I was tired from the travel and probably would have slept through an earthquake. The second night wasn't so good, though. Because the rocks get pounded by wave after wave there's none of that hypnotic sound of the sea regularly lapping the sea shore.

What you get at Storms River is an irregular delivery of large volumes of water plus some howling wind as an accompaniment if you're really unlucky. It's all quite spectacular but it's not conducive to a good night's sleep.

I've made the mistake of holidaying in 'idyllic' spots before and there's generally an unforeseen problem they never mention in the holiday brochures.

As I write this I am looking out over a very attractive bit of Scotland towards Loch Ness. It's a gloriously sunny day and the plan was to have dinner outside this evening because it only gets dark at midnight at this time of year.

The only downside is the midges: the Scottish version of mosquitoes. They don't carry malaria or anything nasty like that, but they do leave small red marks all over your skin when they bite and a swarm of them around your head makes alfresco dining virtually impossible.

Because of the warm April this year there are more than usual, which means that, instead of sitting outside enjoying a few whiskies tonight, we will be shut up indoors.

At least I won't be kept awake by waves crashing onto rocks, though.

Reading the future in Empowermentopia

8 July 2007

Now that John van de Ruit has finally disproved the publishing myth that 4 500 sold copies constitute a bestseller in South Africa, I've decided to write a novel.

Incidentally, what a great bloke Van de Ruit is. I bumped into him at the Book Fair in Cape Town recently and you would never guess from his demeanour that his first novel Spud had sold more than 80 000 copies.

He is charming and modest and has none of the braggadocio sometimes associated with the sort of authors who occasionally make it onto the literary awards short lists.

The front desk staff at the Arabella Sheraton hotel hadn't a clue who he was but my guess is that within a couple of years they will be insisting he stays in a top suite and plying him with Krug and scantily clad models. I hope he remembers to invite me over.

My novel (which will obviously become a runaway bestseller) is set in a fictional country on the southern tip of a fictional continent known internationally for its inability to get its collective act together. It's the year 2010 and the fictional country, called Empowermentopia, has just successfully hosted the Ladies' Underwater Naked Bowls World Cup.

Sadly, the Empowermentopia host team got knocked out in the first round but on the whole everyone is happy because the world said it couldn't be done and Empowermentopia proved the world wrong. An added bonus is that the blazer-wearing executives of the body governing

Ladies' Underwater Naked Bowls cleaned up a small fortune by selling the exclusive rights for coverage to the national broadcaster, the EBC.

The success of the 2010 world championships has briefly taken the minds of the Empowermentopians off the fact that they have a new president.

Swept to power by a populist vote in 2009, he has already stamped his indelible mark on the country. To save court time he has decreed that certain members of society are undesirable and had them imprisoned and tortured. The central jail is full of beaten journalists, cartoonists and newspaper editors seized from their homes by the newly formed Army of Truth at four in the morning.

Homosexuals have been rounded up and used as live targets for shooting practice. Rape cases no longer go to court if the woman was deemed to be wearing provocative clothing. This is not decided by lawyers but by a bunch of presidential cronies over a few beers.

Former political enemies have mysteriously disappeared and it's not uncommon to wake up and hear on state-owned radio that the breaking news story of the morning involves another Mercedes containing a former politician leaving the road at three in the morning and hitting a tree.

The key supporters who swept the new president to power have all been given holiday homes snatched from 'disloyalists' in a highly desirable seaside town. What would pass for bribery and corruption in most other countries is now widely accepted as being the necessary lubricant to keep commerce going.

As we like to say in publishing, all characters are fictional and any resemblance to any persons living or dead is just an unfortunate coincidence.

Let's kill criminals so there's space in prison

15 July 2007

Not surprisingly, the release of those horrific crime figures a couple of weeks ago made front-page headlines in virtually every daily newspaper in the country.

Calls for Charles Nqakula's resignation as Minister of Safety and Security were predictable but what would that achieve? Anyway, nobody ever gets sacked from Thabo Mbeki's Cabinet, however incompetent or mediocre their performance.

A more intelligent approach would be to encourage the poor minister and tell him that he can't even think of resigning until crime levels have dropped substantially.

I was greatly encouraged by the announcement of the crime figures. A few months ago the government wasted an enormous amount of energy claiming that violent crime was a figment of the white imagination; another sign that colonial dinosaurs had refused to embrace the new South Africa. Whingers were told to pack up and leave the country. So the public admission from the minister that crime is out of control (my phrase, not his) is brave and encouraging, particularly bearing in mind that we have so much to lose if Fifa eventually decides that South Africa is too dangerous, even for football fans, and hands the 2010 World Cup to Iraq. Incidentally, I reckon we should sponsor the entire 2010 trip for fans on the understanding that they would patrol the streets at night and show criminals what real violence is all about.

Now that the ANC has finally acknowledged that there is a problem, what does it propose to do about it? The first thing to do would be to re-introduce the death penalty. Those opposed to the death penalty claim it is barbaric but it's certainly no more barbaric than having boiling water poured over you or shooting young children for fun. I have the greatest respect for the judges of the Constitutional Court but on the subject of the death penalty we need a national referendum. We could do this through Vodacom and the proceeds from all the SMSs could be used to build gallows. Our crime situation is so appalling that it would be a pity to limit the death penalty to murder. Since the prisons are overflowing I would suggest a flexible system when it comes to imposing the death penalty. If the prisons are full, then impose the death penalty on a variety of violent crimes until the prison population drops.

Too many cases never come to court due to smart-arse lawyers finding loopholes such as the defendant's name being spelt incorrectly. Where possible, police should be encouraged to shoot armed criminals at the scene of the crime.

Defending your property against armed robbers is illegal in South Africa. I've even been told that I should put up a notice in all official languages warning intruders that the long spikes recently installed on my perimeter walls have been smeared with a lethal toad venom.

Those still advocating a gun-free SA clearly haven't been shot lately. Every householder should be allowed to bear arms and to kill an intruder after a warning shot. Protecting one's property should be recognised as a fundamental human right, particularly in a country like South Africa. The only possible exception would be if the government could guarantee our safety.

Front-row seats at the Mad Bob Show

22 July 2007

One of the great benefits of the Zimbabwean economic meltdown is the opportunity it has given South Africans to watch what can happen to a once-thriving economy if you put a lunatic in charge.

Even on Sunday, staff were busy refilling the shelves of my local supermarket with all manner of fresh fruit and veg. Fellow shoppers were enjoying expensive designer coffees at pavement restaurants and a new patisserie was doing brisk trade in all sorts of yummy treats that could hardly be classed as basic foodstuffs.

Less than 1 000 km away, as the vulture flies, things are very different. The Mad Bob Mugabe half-price sale has emptied shelves of anything and everything if we are to believe the news reports. Despite protestations from the usual Zimbabwean gangsters and the predictable lack of interest on the part of our own dismally inept Ministry of Home Affairs (which hasn't noticed any increase in the flow of Zimbabweans coming to South Africa), I think we can believe the images we have seen on television and in the papers.

I don't think the arrests of Zimbabwean businessmen are fictional and I'm pretty sure you can meet a recently arrived Zimbabwean in South Africa who will confirm the horror stories.

When great tsunamis and powerful hurricanes wreck entire cities and destroy people's lives we can smugly turn on our televisions, watch up-to-the-minute coverage and thank our lucky stars we aren't there.

The recent floods in England made great viewing. People were wading waist-deep through smelly floodwater in places like Sheffield and Don-caster, their homes ruined. As the waters subsided, the TV crews went out to interview people about the damage. One poor couple returned to their flooded home and went into the kitchen. Every electrical device was waterlogged and the wife opened a drawer that was full of kitchen uten-sils swimming in filthy brown water.

It was real rubber-neck television and the final kick in the crotch came with the admission that the couple weren't insured. A great schaden-freude moment.

There are many theories on happiness and one suggests that com-paring ourselves with someone worse off makes us happy. This doesn't make us sound like a very pleasant species but maybe the converse is also true. If we are forced to live with people who have much more than we do, then maybe that makes us unhappy. That may help explain the obscene rush for free money we have witnessed over the past few years.

The television networks know that showing people's lives being ru-ined, whether by war, by natural disaster or on a reality show, is good for the ratings. We love watching the public humiliation of those who can't really sing or somebody covered in insect bites cracking up in a steamy jungle.

Zimbabwe makes us feel good because we aren't there. It's a freak show run by one of the most repulsive men to have ever lived and we have the best seats. What will Mad Bob do next, we wonder.

Whatever it is, it is sure to be newsworthy and it will make us even happier not to be there. But be warned. The Mad Bob Show has enjoyed a long, uninterrupted run and it may soon be coming to a theatre near you. Viva SACP, viva.

Ask not what your President is doing

29 July 2007

A sk not what your country can do for you – ask what you can do for your country.

These are the famous words of John F Kennedy at his inaugural address in 1961 and, despite the laboured syntax, the sentiment is pretty clear.

If President Thabo Mbeki were to say something similar to South Africans today I wonder what our reaction would be. My guess is that we would snort with disbelief and ignore him.

Since liberation in 1994 dozens of ANC cronies have helped themselves to piles of public money, there are innumerable stories of rigged public tenders and there is such a general stench of dishonesty in the air that it would be laughable for the President to tell us to put the country before ourselves.

The unlikeable Ronald Suresh Roberts hasn't managed, with his proctological prose, to convince many critics of the native intelligence of the President.

Perhaps this is because we all know that a large banking group paid Mr Roberts a tidy sum to produce an 'acceptable' book. Let's face it, Absa would hardly have shelled out a million and a half if it thought the book was going to highlight the President's inability (or unwillingness?) to spot a human rights tragedy in the making in Zimbabwe or dwell on his curious management style which encourages mediocrity rather than excellence.

I'm told by cynical business friends that if you want to stay at the top you should surround yourself with sycophants and people who don't have the type of skills that might threaten you. This has worked very well for Mbeki, since the ANC way of doing things demands that everyone must loyally follow the same line.

So, if the President talks nonsense about HIV/Aids then it is expected that everyone else will talk the same nonsense. Thankfully, we have a handful of Cabinet ministers who are brave enough to voice a more intelligent point of view from time to time, but they are sadly in the minority.

The ANC's succession race is another interesting example of its passion for mediocrity. Never slow to tell business how to run its affairs, the ruling party hasn't managed to produce a credible successor to Mbeki.

I suspect that this has more to do with the idiosyncratic ways of the ANC than it has to do with the lack of potential candidates. Apparently it's regarded as very bad manners to make your ambitions known in the ANC. To stand up at a party conference and say you believe you have the necessary qualities to lead this country to greatness is akin to farting in a departing lift in the eyes of the ANC.

This is odd because a successful company is always looking for new talent and devising ways to encourage and hold on to it. In the ANC, it seems, you have to have meetings behind closed doors and jockey for position while making it quite clear you are not ambitious.

Whatever that is, it isn't democracy, which is why the ANC finds itself in the embarrassing position of possibly having to consider a third term for Mbeki.

As the country slides further towards anarchy and crime begins to cause a mass exodus of transferable skills, wouldn't it be wonderful to have the sort of president who could ask us what we can do for our country and be taken seriously?

A handy lesson in brainwashing

5 August 2007

The scenes of the Putin youth all dressed in red T-shirts and shouting for their leader at the Lake Seliger resort reminded me of film footage I have seen of the Hitler Youth.

In case you haven't a clue what I'm talking about, let me fill you in. Nashi, a pro-Kremlin youth group (funded by the Kremlin, you won't be surprised to hear) has just hosted a summer camp for about 10 000 young Russians to encourage them to be loyal to their leader and their country. They start the day with mass exercise, then head off to do wholesome things like play volleyball, sail boats or cycle.

Vocal Kremlin critics, such as chess champion Garry Kasparov, are depicted as prostitutes with pictures of their faces attached to pictures of the bodies of scantily clad women.

The happy campers live in a pristine woodland environment, but there are two grim wooden shacks surrounded by broken glass for the supporters of 'The Other Russia', a coalition that is critical of the Kremlin. It may be very unsubtle propaganda but it works and nobody getting a free lakeside holiday from the Kremlin is likely to complain.

Not surprisingly, many of the young people come from lower-income families, which makes them far more impressionable than those with enough monetary independence to allow them to make their own choices as to whether the Kremlin is doing a good job.

Booze is banned in the camp but sex is encouraged, it seems. Russia is trying to reverse a fall in the population and is actively encouraging Kremlin supporters to reproduce. According to one newspaper report, 39 couples will marry at the camp. If you're really naive you may just manage to convince yourself that all this is no different from the summer camps run in the West.

If you're rather more cynical you may well find in it something far more sinister than even Britain's Young Conservatives.

President Putin doesn't seem to be the sort of man who takes criticism well. So part of his solution has been to vilify his political opponents and give a free holiday to 10 000 kids, who are probably gullible enough to believe all the propaganda and who will form a formidable and unquestioning support base for the future. Like the Hitler Youth, the infallibility of the great leader and the need for patriotism are doled out in equal measure.

I wonder whether the ANC shouldn't try a similar strategy. Admittedly, the weather has been pretty lousy of late, but September should be rather more clement and an ideal opportunity to take 10 000 still previously disadvantaged youngsters away to Lake Suresh for a weekend's appreciation of the great leader. Pictures of Messrs Owen, Bullard, Makhanya and Donaldson could be superimposed onto pictures of the bodies of transvestite hijackers and paraded around.

Lectures on how best to trash the classier suburbs when protesting or on how to recognise a coconut would be given daily, with a speciality course offered on how to befriend dodgy businessmen and get them to buy you a fast sports car. Naturally, free kangas would be available for all female campers.

Not that far from the madding crowd

12 August 2007

The reassuring voice of Talk Radio 702's award-winning journalist Stephen Grootes urged me not to panic buy petrol when the first real signs of a looming fuel shortage became apparent.

It was probably the worst advice ever offered by a talk-show host in the history of the world.

The normally sensible Grootes' view was that if none of us panicked there would be plenty left for everyone and an emergency could therefore be averted. He obviously isn't familiar with popular delusion and the madness of crowds.

Fortunately I ignored his advice and, like most of my neighbours, immediately drove to my local petrol station and topped up a half-empty tank.

At the end of a normal tank fill the pump jockey will usually take ages to squeeze a few rands worth of petrol into the tank. It's an irritating and time-wasting habit but on my last fill up I was in a time-wasting mood.

We even rocked the car backwards and forwards in an attempt to fill the tank to the brim. I could see that people in the long queue behind me were beginning to get agitated so I decided to get the tyre pressures checked while I was there.

After all, what's the point in being at the front of a petrol queue during a fuel crisis and not making the most of it?

Then we held a red alert meeting at home and decided that only absolutely essential journeys would be undertaken until supplies could be guaranteed.

We also did a bit of scenario planning and reckoned that a nationwide fuel shortage would also eventually affect food deliveries. So we went in for some panic food buying as well (sorry Stephen). Essentials like long-life milk, wildebeest paté, Belgian chocolate and oat cakes. Cooking oil is usually the first thing to run out when a food shortage occurs so we bought some just in case, even though we don't use it. If things get really bad we can probably swap it for biltong.

My first thought on discovering queues at the petrol stations was for those poor Zimbabwean illegal immigrants flooding into our beautiful country at a rate of 6 000 a day. They have crawled through the dust under barbed wire in their ragged clothes, pausing only to be filmed by the Sky News crew.

They have been picked up by burly white farmers in bakkies, had their hands tied and been sent back across the border. Still desperately hungry, lonely and scared they have crawled once again under the barbed wire, deciding this time to avoid the Sky News film crew, and finally made the long and difficult journey to the promised land of Gauteng.

And what do they find when they arrive? Long queues for petrol, rioting in the townships, no water and frequent power cuts.

First impressions are very important, whether one is arriving at OR Tambo Airport for a five-week sojourn in our top resorts or whether one is part of a mass exodus from the wreckage of a neighbouring state.

The psychological damage when Zimbabwean refugees discover this country is no different from Zimbabwe will be immense. On the other hand, maybe it will persuade some of them to go back home again thus averting the humanitarian crisis the ANC fails to recognise anyway.

It's no secret that fools are gullible

19 August 2007

I t's a frightening thought that a book called *The Secret* is currently the number one bestseller in the non-fiction category in this country.

Equally frightening is the fact that Sir Richard Branson's *Screw It* self-help books occupy second and third place – but that's a topic for another day.

We have come a long way in the past 2 000 years. We have bottled water, flat-screen TVs, iPods, cars that automatically turn on the windscreen wipers when it rains and multiple-personality cellphones. We even have Paris Hilton. None of these existed 2 000 years ago – they didn't even exist 50 years ago. A thousand years ago most people couldn't write so it was up to the scholars and wise men (who could write) to tell the rest of mankind what to do and how to behave.

For example, gods have never spoken directly to common men. They have always dealt through earthly intermediaries who, for some reason, have been considerably better dressed, better housed and better fed than the people they have to talk to. The old idea of good people going to heaven and bad people going to hell would have fallen a little flat in print but commission a large painting for the back of the church and people soon get the message.

Be meek and obedient and obey orders and ye shall follow the white line up to the clouds with people playing harps and having a good time. Be naughty and disobedient and ye shall follow the black line down to the fiery pit where people with scaly legs and fish heads poke you all day with a pitchfork and everyone (apart from the torturers that is) seems to be having a really lousy time; and for eternity to boot.

Not surprisingly, simple and superstitious folk who relied on the feudal lord for survival didn't want to take any chances and opted for the meek and obedient way. The point is that they didn't know any better. They couldn't read and even if they could have they wouldn't have had access to very many books.

People's inability to question authority or even allow themselves the luxury of independent thought are the reasons most people are subjugated, whether they know it or not. These days there is little excuse for remaining superstitious and ignorant. There are plenty of reference books available, there are authoritative TV documentaries and there is the ultimate educator, the Internet.

Within minutes you can learn all about the disease you've just been diagnosed with and join a chat room full of fellow sufferers. You can Google virtually any subject and get a selection of pretty reliable pages to increase your knowledge. If ever there was an age where superstition and stupidity are severely threatened it should be now.

Then along comes *The Secret*, which panders to man's most basic instincts: greed, envy and sloth. According to the book all you have to do is visualise what you want and the universe will deliver it without you having to do a thing.

Did you ever hear such codswallop and can you believe that otherwise sane people are buying this book and going home to wish themselves a new S Class Mercedes-Benz? As the priests discovered 1 000 years ago, desperate people are gullible people and nothing seems to have changed. So maybe I'll buy the book and visualise a new president ...

Government bully terrorises business

26 August 2007

As any good school bully will tell you, bullying is an art. It's not simply a matter of picking on the kid with the big teeth and silly glasses
or pinching other people's pocket money in the playground.

No, it's much more strategic. Ideally, the bully won't pick on someone
who is obviously weaker because that's too easy and, besides, it looks too
much like bullying. So the ideal victim is someone who looks as though
he might be able to stand up for himself but can be worn down by con-
tinual and relentless pressure.

Then there's the matter of whether to go for physical or psychological
bullying. Physical bullying is very straightforward and involves hitting
someone who is unlikely to hit back. It's the lowest form of the art and
its proponents are not held in high esteem.

Psychological bullying, on the other hand, requires careful planning
but its rewards are greater. Smack a smaller kid in the playground and
all you have is a blubbing child and an angry parent.

Make an unwilling victim stand on a desk in front of his peers and
sing the national anthem in a falsetto voice and you may well have damaged someone for life.

One is about physical pain and the other is about mental pain. The
dedicated bully delights in the discomfort of his victims and their public
humiliation. Occasionally the victim will crack and fight back, but most
know there's no point because what is happening to them isn't seen by

teachers or parents as conventional bullying.

There are no bruises to show as evidence and if they go running home to mummy complaining that they've been humiliated they will only be told to stand up for themselves and stop being a sissy.

Our employment law is a fine example of psychological bullying. The victim in this case is the terrified figure of big business and the bully is the government. The government wants to show everyone that it has the loudest voice in the playground so it tells big business how to behave. Big business has been running its operations quite successfully for years, but the problem is that the wrong sort of people have been benefiting. So the government has said that it's time big business changed its ways and employed different-coloured people, plus a few one-legged whale-loving lesbians just for good measure. In addition, it must hand over half its lunch money so that people who haven't had lunch before can now do so. If it doesn't do this, hints the government, then it won't be big business for very much longer.

Big business realises there's no way out so it employs different-coloured people just as it's told. The only problem is that there aren't enough different-coloured people who know what they're doing and big business meekly says so. Not a problem, says the government, which knows bugger all about how to run a business, employ them anyway.

Just when big business thinks it has satisfied all the bully's ridiculous conditions, the bully thinks of new ones such as insisting that 35% of all board meetings are held in an African language. Eventually big business becomes too scared to go to school, which leaves the government with no one left to bully.

Wagner runs rings around SA politics

2 September 2007

Watching seven Wagner operas over a period of 10 days is, admittedly, not everyone's idea of a blissful annual holiday, but that's what I've been up to these past couple of weeks.

Richard Wagner was a sort of 19th century version of Mick Jagger with a bit of Sol Kerzner thrown in; he wanted complete control over the performance of his operas, or music dramas as he preferred them to be known, so he built his own opera house in a nondescript town called Bayreuth in Bavaria.

Unlike Jagger, Wagner didn't have enough money, so he got the local nutty monarch, King Ludwig II, to sign the cheques in his quest for an acoustically perfect opera house.

Every year Bayreuth opens and hosts a season of Wagner's music dramas. No other composer's operas are ever performed there, although Beethoven's ninth was performed with Wagner's approval, and American musicals were put on there at the end of World War Two for the amusement of the liberation troops. The annual Wagner festival is still administered by the composer's family and would have fallen foul of South African political correctness laws years ago: there is no talk of empowerment; not even of letting a member of the Strauss or Puccini family have a go one year. It is a jealously guarded fiefdom, which means that the fights for control (and there are many) take place between members of the Wagner family.

Tickets for the Bayreuth festival are hard to come by; demand exceeds supply by a factor of nine. Consequently, there is a high secondary market price for tickets. My wife went on the Internet and discovered that we could sell our entire ticket allocation and make enough profit to buy a new VW Golf GTi for cash. This is the sort of behaviour which, if discovered, gets you blacklisted for life and explains why certain members of the ANC will never be seen at Bayreuth.

Obviously we resisted the temptation to make a fast buck, although I briefly wondered whether that had been such a good decision, three hours into *Siegfried*.

So we sat it out, through all seven operas, in the knowledge that almost a quarter of a million rands had evaporated over the past 10 days.

Wagner's magnum opus is something called the *Ring of the Nibelung*. It consists of four operas performed over four nights and the whole thing lasts for around 14 hours. It's about many things, but central to its theme is the renunciation of love in return for power. The power comes from a hoard of magic gold stolen from some careless Rhine-maiden security guards by a thuggish dwarf called Alberich, a previously disadvantaged Nibelung.

This annoys the ruling class of gods headed by a one-eyed boss called Wotan, and they expend a lot of energy tricking Alberich out of the gold. Whoever has the gold has the power, so a couple of giants demand the gold from the gods as payment for building Wotan's new Tuscan golf estate, and once they have it one giant kills the other in a fit of jealousy and turns himself into a dragon to defend the precious gold.

If that all sounds suspiciously like South African politics, don't worry, it's supposed to. That's the timeless genius of Wagner.